KURILPA BRIDGE

HAIG BECK AND JACKIE COOPER

Published in Australia in 2012 by
The Images Publishing Group Pty Ltd
ABN 89 059 734 431
6 Bastow Place, Mulgrave, Victoria 3170, Australia
Tel: +61 3 9561 5544 Fax: +61 3 9561 4860
books@imagespublishing.com
www.imagespublishing.com

National Library of Australia Cataloguing-in-Publication entry:

Title:	Kurilpa Bridge
Authors:	Haig Beck and Jackie Cooper
Contributors:	Cox Architects
Editor:	Debbie Ball
ISBN:	9781864704082 (hbk.)
Subjects:	Cable-stayed bridges – Queensland – Brisbane.
	Footbridges – Queensland – Brisbane.
	Kurilpa Bridge (Brisbane, Qld.)

Dewey Number: 624.238099431

Pre-publishing services by Mission Productions Limited, Hong Kong
Printed on 150gsm Quatro Silk Matt paper by Everbest Printing Co. Ltd., in Hong Kong/China

IMAGES has included on its website a page for special notices in relation to this and our other
publications. Please visit www.imagespublishing.com.

CONTENTS

PREFATORY REMARKS

Our background is writing about architecture, not civil engineering: what do we know about bridge design? Yet the Kurilpa Bridge has excited much comment; and unravelling the story behind its design has been intriguing and rewarding. To untutored eyes, the supporting structure does not make sense: the seemingly chaotic cables, the spiky, stick-like masts and the improbable thinness of the central span, defy any structural logic we are familiar with. Bridge designers usually make a big point of expressing how their bridges work. They clearly expose the structural principles in play, and you don't have to be an engineer to see how the load is transferred to each side and why the bridges don't fall down. The Kurilpa Bridge doesn't do this. It has disturbed and teased our expectations.

This bridge has been widely represented as the 'first tensegrity bridge'. As baby boomers, we know something about tensegrity structures, having sat at the feet (literally, for several hours) of one of our generation's design gurus, R Buckminster Fuller, in the 1970s and listened to him expound on 'finite resources', 'spaceship earth', 'geodesic domes' and 'tensegrity structures'. Bucky was one of a kind, the first engineer to spread the word about the earth's dwindling resources and the need for recycling and doing more with less. We remember from his lectures that tensegrity structures are very efficient but their practical application was largely limited to geodesic domes. The compression members – 'sticks' – are all segregated by the tension members – 'cables'. The result is a spider's web of cables, with sticks appearing to float in mid-air. The Kurilpa Bridge exhibits some members that are part of a tensegrity structure, but clearly it's not a pure tensegrity structure.

If you Google 'Kurilpa Bridge', you'll get over 14,000 entries, most of them internet chaff. We sifted through some of this and found an interesting site, a blog by the 'Happy Pontist', who wasn't too happy with le Pont de Kurilpa: 'irrational, visually chaotic, disruptive, and possibly one of the most expensive fixed footbridges ever built'. (We are reliably informed that the Pontist's cost estimate was wrong by a factor of more than two – making the Kurilpa Bridge in fact one of the more economical of recently built large-span footbridges.) Nor was the Pontist too pleased with a hybrid structure that 'appears to be based on tensegrity geometries, but it's not strictly a tensegrity bridge at all … it's a complex variant on the good old cable-stayed bridge, [with] a substantial dash of the inverted fink truss thrown in.' The Pontist explains his point of view: 'Like many bridge engineers, I like a bridge where the structural principles are clear and comprehensible … But I do admire its audacity, the willingness to install something that works against the orthogonality of its surroundings; a provocation which offers restlessness in place of reassurance.'

As design critics, we appreciate such succinctly expressed prejudices. They expose heuristics at work.

A *heuristic* (from the Greek: 'to find' or 'discover') describes the application of a rule of thumb, an educated guess, or common sense. There are negative and positive heuristics. A negative heuristic forbids the designer from asking certain questions for fear they may unleash a swarm of anomalies. The Happy Pontist identifies this risk when he (she?) admits the possibility of 'something that works against the orthogonality of its surroundings; a provocation which offers restlessness in place of reassurance'. Similarly, there is a negative heuristic behind the view that would regard the hybrid structure as transgressive; or that sees the bridge as 'irrational, visually chaotic, disruptive'. On the other hand, a positive heuristic provides a designer with rules for avoiding the risk of a swarm of anomalies by establishing principles that ignore counter-examples, as in: 'I like a bridge where the structural principles are clear and comprehensible'.

The identification of such heuristics raises the questions: How did these heuristics come about? Why do they persist? Are they valid?

In addressing questions such as these, the critic enters into a contract with the reader. Instead of declaiming from on high (this is 'good', that is 'bad'), the critic's duty – as we see it – is to develop a context that will enable readers to make their own informed value judgements. Of course, as critics we begin this task with certain prejudices of our own already in place, and readers should know something of these at the outset.

We subscribe to a view best expressed by the architectural historian and theorist, Joseph Rykwert: 'There cannot be design without artifice'. And 'The artifice of transforming brute matter into built statement must … be subject to the rules of some game'.

The critic's duty – as we see it – is to develop a context that will enable readers to make their own informed judgements

Furthermore, the belief that design can make human existence meaningful beyond fulfilling practical needs is an idea that resonates with us.

We have applied these core ideas to our writings on contemporary architecture, jewellery, sculpture and environmental graphics, as we do here to bridge design.

The text that follows is arranged in four parts, which can be read as separate essays in any order: 'Kurilpa Bridge', a description and discussion of the bridge; 'Hybridity and Chaos', an enquiry into the aesthetic systems evident in the design of the bridge; 'Bridge Art', which explores the relationship between bridge design, applied art and art; and 'An Abridged History', a brief and partial history of bridges. While many people have a fair grasp of the history of art and architecture, fewer know much about the history of bridges. We felt it necessary to tell this history in order to understand Kurilpa Bridge in context.

In developing these texts, we have assimilated facts from many sources. In doing so, we make no pretence to scholarship, so you will find no footnotes. Where we are indebted to someone for an idea, we have acknowledged them in the body of the text. And where ideas have been amply expressed by others, we have left it to those authors to speak.

Haig Beck and Jackie Cooper
Point Lookout, March 2011

KURILPA BRIDGE

HAIG BECK AND JACKIE COOPER

The Kurilpa Bridge is lauded as 'one of the most audacious and technically ambitious bridge designs of recent years…'

South Bank is Brisbane's beating cultural heart, alive with tourists and students, visitors down from the country, families out for a day, young people enjoying a night on the town, people dressed to the nines for the theatre, and street kids hanging out. It is a riverside parkland filled with fine civic buildings: museums, art galleries, theatres, an opera house and concert hall, music conservatorium and art school. In the streets nearby, a vast exhibition and conference centre, cinemas, university campuses, entertainment venues, new hotels, restaurants, street cafes, stylish bars and small shops.

At each end of this reach of the Brisbane River, book-ending the contemporary culture park, are two dramatic pedestrian bridges. They launch themselves over the river, penetrate the tangle of expressways that stretch along the northern bank, and land in the city. The bridges unite the two sides of Brisbane and establish an uninterrupted circuit through the city. A *flâneur* may wander from the city with its shops and pavement cafes, via the Goodwill Bridge across the river and through the South Bank riverside parkland, following the sinuous path of the Grand Arbour draped in purple bougainvillea, past concert halls and art galleries, then spiral up and back across the river over Kurilpa Bridge.

The Kurilpa Bridge is lauded as 'one of the most audacious and technically ambitious bridge designs of recent years … a unique urban landmark to rival the London Millennium Bridge'. The bridge is a giant 'cat's cradle' of stainless steel cables and very large white 'pickup sticks' suspended across the river, in defiance of gravity and all known rules of bridge building. Most bridge engineers prefer the structural principles of a bridge to be clear and comprehensible. They want their bridges to show how they stand up, and how they work, so that when you cross them you know why they won't collapse. But not the designers of the Kurilpa Bridge. Their bridge is quite disruptive. Seemingly irrational and visually chaotic, its spiky web structure offers a tensed counterpoise to the rectilinear city skyline beyond.

A CITY DIVIDED

Brisbane was not always joined by bridges. It was once a city divided by the river. And long before the first settlement by convicts in 1825, the river divided the Aboriginal people: to the north of the river were the Turrbal people; and to the south, the Jagera. On the south bank of the river was Kurilpa ('Kuril's place'), an area stretching upriver from Victoria Bridge that we now know as West End. (For the Turrbal people, the Kuril dreaming is a love story about a Dilly Bag Girl whose totem was the kangaroo marsupial rat.) The area was a neutral meeting place for these tribes and a rich food-gathering place. 'Aboriginal [people] … swam from North Brisbane to the sandy beaches at the bend in the river to fish, to gather yam and reeds from the swamps, and to hunt rats and scrub turkeys in what constituted the West End jungle.'

'The jungle was a tangled mass: of trees, vines, flowering creepers, staghorns, elkhorns, towering scrub palms, giant ferns and hundreds of other varieties of the fern family, beautiful and rare orchids, and the wild passion flower. While along the riverbank were the water lilies in thousands, and convolvulus [morning glory] of gorgeous hue … Parrots, blue pigeons and scrub turkeys could be seen in the rainforest itself, where the whip birds gave their distinctive call …' (from an ex-convict's notes of the 1820's).

Convicts soon cleared this paradisical rainforest, sweeping away the bora rings and other signs of Aboriginal culture, to plant market gardens on the fertile river flats. In 1838 the Moreton Bay Settlement was opened to free settlers. Squatters on the Darling Downs began sending their wool for shipping out of Brisbane. Coming from the Downs, the wool drays kept to bush tracks on the south side of the river. Those tracks led to South Bank, where wool stores and wharves were built. The squattocracy followed the wool and built townhouses in what is now fashionable West End. For their recreation, they laid out a racetrack in the Melbourne Street swamp. South Brisbane was a bustling port and its streets thronged with sailors, recently arrived immigrants, visiting squatters, teamsters, travellers from the bush, and local businessmen and working people. They all gave the south side of the river a raffish quality that divided it socially from the more sedate north side, with its bureaucrats in government offices.

THE RECONNECTED CITY

A timber bridge linking the two sides of the river was built in 1865. Attacked by marine borers, it collapsed only two years later. An iron bridge replaced it in 1874. It, in turn, was swept away in the 1893 floods. In 1897 the old Victoria Bridge was erected in its place (to be replaced in 1969 by the present Victoria Bridge). Throughout this period, the connection between the two sides of the river remained tenuous, even after the William Jolly (Grey Street) Bridge was opened in 1932.

Following the 1893 floods, businesses shifted to higher ground on the northern side of the river and stayed there. As transport systems improved, commerce continued to decline on the southern side. During World War II, General MacArthur segregated black American soldiers on the seedy south side of the river. In the 1970s and 80s things improved: the blighted South Bank became the site for a series of important cultural buildings and the venue of World Expo 88. Redevelopment of the Expo site into riverside parkland became the catalyst for the reinvigoration of the surrounding streets.

The Goodwill Bridge and CBD from South Bank
Victoria Bridge (built: 1969)
Grey Street Bridge (built: 1932)
Victoria Bridge (built: 1897)
Victoria Bridge (built: 1874)

Brisbane Convention and Exhibition Centre (1996) also by Cox Rayner and Arup. South Brisbane reach of the Brisbane River from the south

Sydney Opera House, engineered by Arup (1973)

Brisbane's Story Bridge, built by Baulderstone Hornibrook (1940)

In 1995, Michael Rayner, of Cox Rayner Architects, was working on the Brisbane City Centre Strategy Plan. He proposed a series of river crossings to join the two halves of the city and provide opportunities to reduce the dominance of cars. Rayner envisaged the city reconnected along the length of its fat serpentine river, offering pedestrians new ways of accessing the city and celebrating an outdoors urban lifestyle: Brisbane might redefine itself as a subtropical city. As a first step he suggested a pedestrian and cycle link across the Brisbane River from South Bank to the CBD peninsula. The Queensland Government welcomed the idea and in 1999 a design and construct competition for the bridge was held. The winning scheme was designed by Cox Rayner, engineered by Arup and built by John Holland. Named the Goodwill Bridge and opened in 2001, it was the first link in Rayner's vision for Brisbane.

PEDESTRIAN BRIDGE POETICS

Traffic engineers should not be permitted to design pedestrian bridges: they seek to achieve order and efficiency for traffic. Pedestrians needs are different: they do not move through the city in metal boxes sealed off from the world, and they are not always looking for the quickest route between A and B. Pedestrians have the luxury, if they wish, of being able to amble through city streets and parks, across busy intersections and down deserted lanes, through patches of sunshine and pools of shade. They smell the hot pavement after rain, hear the cacophony of street sounds and feel the sudden blasts of cold air as automatic doors slide open on passing buses. For the pedestrian who is not in too great a hurry, the city is a place of sensual experiences, taken for granted no doubt, but nevertheless available to be enjoyed.

For the pedestrian, bridges have a special, even poetic dimension. In a physical but also a mystical sense, a bridge connects separate realms. The Pontiff of Rome is for Roman Catholics the bridge between God and man. Pontiff derives from *Pontifex*, Latin for 'builder of bridges'. The word originates from Roman antiquity, when the Tiber was a sacred river and a god, and only those of the highest status were permitted to build bridges, a process attended by magic rites and propitiation.

To cross a bridge is to be suspended physically between two banks and existentially between two realms. Existentially, bridges symbolise the transition from one state to another, change or the desire for change. To cross a bridge is to embark on an adventure.

Like the Goodwill Bridge, the Kurilpa Bridge prolongs the pleasure of being between two realms, by stretching the journey and providing moments to savour the experience. The trip across the bridge is linear, but not direct. Like all good travelogues, the crossing in either direction is episodic and different: there is a beginning, along the way there are twists and turns and some revelations and surprises, and there is an end.

From the northern side of the river, the bridge initially has the characteristics of a pedestrian overpass (which at this point in the journey it is). Resembling a partially enclosed concrete ramp, the engineering drama is not immediately disclosed. Only on turning a bend is this progressively revealed; and even then, as an overhead performance of structural gymnastics. The purpose of all the sticks and cables is not clear, and they have no immediate bearing on any understanding of how the bridge is held up. In contrast, from the approach along the southern bank of the river, the structural histrionics of the bridge are in plain view, especially the apparently gravity-defying river spans. From this bank one embarks on the crossing fully aware that somehow it is these sticks and cables that hold up the bridge.

To cross a bridge is to embark on an adventure

KURILPA BRIDGE ORIGINS

Shortly after the Goodwill Bridge was opened, Michael Rayner and his office undertook a competition for the design of the Brisbane Magistrates Court. While exploring the relationship of the Court to its larger urban context, Rayner drew an axis on the line of Tank Street running through the Court site. On a larger map it could be seen that extending this axis would establish a continuous pedestrian link between the Roma Street Parklands in the north, across the river to South Bank and beyond to West End. Cox Rayner incorporated this idea in the competition entry, identifying the end of Tank Street as a site for a second pedestrian bridge. The government incorporated the idea into the City Centre Master Plan. A budget was developed and Cabinet approved a competition for the design and construction of the Tank Street Bridge, announced in late 2006.

The Cox Rayner/Arup/Baulderstone team (formed for the competition) was experienced and has already worked together on large construction projects. Cox Rayner has designed some of Brisbane's largest public buildings, including the Brisbane Convention and Exhibition Centre (1994) and the new Brisbane Magistrates Court (2000–06). Arup, an international firm of engineers and design consultants, were the structural designers for the Sydney Opera House (1957–73), the Centre Pompidou in Paris (1971–77) and the Beijing Water Cube (2006–08). They worked with Cox Rayner on the design of the Goodwill Bridge. Baulderstone are world-famous bridge builders whose projects include Brisbane's Story Bridge (1935–40) and the Puente Centenario over the Panama Canal (2002–04). The Baulderstone team recall how 'usually a bridge design arrives in our office completed and we have to work out how to build it, which can be very tricky when it comes to large-span structures. So being part of the design team was for us extremely exciting.' The team set about designing the bridge.

HOW TO DESIGN A BRIDGE

How do you design a bridge? While most bridges look different, they are all based on a limited number of structural types. Bridge design therefore begins with choosing the structural type best suited to the required span and the site conditions. In the case of the Tank Street Bridge, the navigation channel determined the main span, was most of the width of the river: about 100 metre. (In the final design, the bridge is angled across the river and the main span is 128 metre.) For this order of span, there is only a handful of suitable structural types:

– a mast on the CBD side with cables radiating down to support the bridge deck
– a mast on the South Bank side
– an arch with the deck suspended from it
– the deck supported by a suspension structure
  (like a miniature Golden Gate Bridge)
– a tube encasing the deck
– a truss.

... bridges are all based on a limited number of structural types

There are other types, but they were immediately excluded from consideration because of the particularities of the site. The landing point on the Tank Street side of the river is 10 metre higher than the South Bank side. This difference is aggravated by a navigation requirement for an 11 metre clearance at high water for the full width of the navigation channel (which at this point on the river stretches virtually from one bank to the other), and over 5 metre clearance above the Riverside Expressway

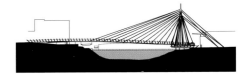
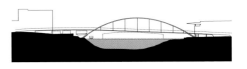
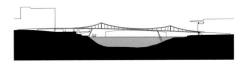

Cable structure with mast on CBD side
Cable structure with mast on South Bank side
Arched bridge
Suspension bridge
Tube bridge

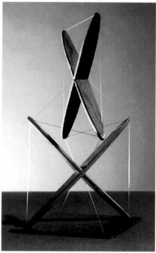

Victoria Bridge with its deep supporting beams

Kenneth Snelson's X-Piece (1949) – one of the inspirations for the development of tensegrity structures

Richard Buckminster Fuller with a tensegrity structure

and North Quay. The required clearances could be easily achieved on the Tank Street side with a gentle ramp, but on the South Bank side a fall of nearly 13 metres had to be accommodated, from the highest point of the deck above the expressway to the South Bank landing. The structure supporting the bridge deck needs to be as thin as possible over the river and the Expressway: the deeper this structure is, the higher the bridge deck will be, and the longer the length of the ramp required to get down to the ground. This ramp would also have to turn back on itself to arrive at the natural access point to the bridge from the public walkway that follows the river's edge.

The team now rejected another bridge type – a beam structure located under the deck – because of the considerable depth of a beam needed to span the river. (The nearby Victoria Bridge has 'beams' that are graceful arches, quite shallow in the centre, but necessarily very deep at the ends from where they spring.) The team also decided that in Brisbane's fierce summer sunshine and afternoon thunderstorms, people should cross the river walking under a street verandah. Any design would require a structure that could support not only the deck, but also an awning.

Sketch designs were developed for five bridge types and these were tested against structural, functional and aesthetic criteria. All were found wanting. Supporting the awning was a real problem for some types; cost was another factor; the thickness of the deck support structure another. Important too was the issue of an arresting visual identity: all the sketch designs lacked either structural originality (the wow! factor) or the scale and presence to give them landmark significance. The team was at a standstill. Then in one of those serendipitous moments that are a feature in all creative acts, someone said 'What about a tensegrity structure'?

WHAT IS TENSEGRITY?

'The word *tensegrity*', explains the 20th-century American inventor-genius, R Buckminster Fuller, 'is an invention: it is a contraction of *tensional integrity*.' A pure tensegrity structure separates members in tension from those in compression. As structural systems go, it is highly theoretical and of limited practical application.

When structures are loaded, the members are subject to tension and/or compression. Tensile stresses result from pulling and compressive stresses from pushing. A column – when loaded – is in compression. A cable on a suspension bridge, is in tension. A truss is a network of (usually) similar members – some in compression and others in tension – all working in concert. Because each of the members can be seen, it is possible to 'see' the structural task of each member, such as: whether it is resisting pushing or pulling forces. A beam is like a truss but with all the holes between the members filled in; the pulling and pushing forces are still in play, but they can't be 'seen'.

The filled-in holes highlight the issue of efficiency. Nearly all structural design seeks to achieve the desired effect with the least material. Members in compression need to be relatively thick so they don't buckle when loaded, while those in tension can be a lot thinner. Building a structure with both thick and thin members may be efficient in terms of reducing weight (the measure engineers use to gauge the amount of material used) but not in terms of labour. Thick and thin members are based on different technologies, for example: rolled steel sections and steel cables. Mixing different technologies can require complex jointing techniques and specialised fabrication skills, which calls for expert labour, that can be very expensive. So a balance is struck: often all the members will be made from the same material, be similar in size and use the same jointing techniques. This means that some members will end up being bigger than they really need to be.

The beautiful, elegant thing about tensegrity structures, is that the two stresses (the pushing and pulling forces) are separated out: a member is either in pure compression or pure tension. In a tensegrity structure: islands of compression are isolated inside a continuous network of lines of tension. It is easy to identify which is which: members in tension are 'cable-like' and very thin, and the ones in compression are 'stick-like' and relatively thick. A genuine tensegrity structure can be easily identified by the fact that the compression members (the sticks) are only attached to tension members (the cables), with compression members not directly connected to each other.

This formal distinction between tension and compression members (between the cables and the sticks) eliminates the wasteful practice of over-sizing some members; a feature of many other types of structures. Additionally, in a tensegrity structure, the tension members take the shortest route between one compression member and another (these shortest routes between points are said to be 'geodesic'). These characteristics mean that tensegrity structures can be light and structurally efficient. However, this efficiency needs to be balanced against their inherent constructional complexity and the tendency to flex and move under 'live' loads (such as people moving around and the varying pressure of gusting wind). Compared to other structural systems, they are what engineers would term very 'lively', which limits their practical application.

The problem with tensegrity structures, is that as they are loaded, the tension members (the cables) begin to stretch under the force of the added load and the whole assembly of sticks and cables deflects significantly. This makes the accurate calculation of the length, size and location of each member, a difficult exercise. Consequently, tensegrity structures have tended to be empirically designed sculptural oddities, the most famous being the works of the American artist, Kenneth Snelson.

In the Kurilpa Bridge, Arup used tensegrity elements to laterally brace the masts and to support the continuous awning, while using a stiffer and more conventional mast and cable arrangement for the primary support of the bridge deck.

Kenneth Snelson's Needle Tower (1968)
Kenneth Snelson's Easy-K (1970)
Early sketch by Philip Cox of the Kurilpa Bridge
Kurilpa Bridge from William Jolly Bridge (rendering)

A TENSEGRITY BRIDGE?

Engineer, Tristram Carfrae, had proposed a tensegrity structure for the bridge, a ground-breaking engineering design challenge. The bridge builders from Baulderstone, who were on the team, were equally excited by the pioneering engineering and challenges posed in erecting a bridge type so structurally complex, that it had not been attempted before. Rayner looking at a picture of Kenneth Snelson perched high over a pond in Arnhem, Holland, erecting his bridge-like 'Easy-K' tensegrity sculpture (1970), with its 30 metre cantilever, remembers thinking 'Why not'? The tensegrity concept for the bridge was immediately appealing because it answered functional and aesthetic issues, that were problems in the other designs. It allowed the bridge deck depth over the river to be less than a metre, substantially reducing the length of ramp required on the South Bank side. It provided a structural

... tensegrity structures have tended to be empirically designed sculptural oddities

'Designing the bridge, we thought abstractly of contemporary dance and music …'

system with significant aesthetic and landmark qualities. Additionally, the system allowed the structural integration of the awning.

As the design proceeded, Carfrae and the Arup team developed an engineering concept for the bridge using a stiffer mast and cable arrangement (conventionally employed in 'cable-stayed' bridge structures) for the primary support of the bridge deck, tensegrity elements to laterally brace the masts and support the continuous awning.

Cable-stayed bridges consist of a mast (a compression member) and a system of cables (tension members) supporting the bridge deck (also a compression member). Instead of a single mast, a cluster of four asymmetrically opposed 'stick-like' masts were fixed at their bases to concrete piers, located on each side of the navigation channel. At intervals between, the pairs of angled stick-masts, were anchored to the edges of the bridge deck substructure. From the top ends of these 20 compression members run the tension cables. Some to support the bridge deck and others to support a series of 16 almost horizontal tensegrity 'sticks' floating in space above the bridge awning.

No 'stick' is perpendicular to the bridge deck. No two sticks are at the same angle and the cables seem to run in all directions. This apparent disorder runs counter to the bridge design convention, that the structural principles be clear and comprehensible. Even an engineer, might at first, be troubled when trying to work out what holds what up. For the rest of us, it is near impossible to derive the sense of a coherent structural system.

And this seems to have been the objective of the designers: to make the bridge as a contemporary art work. It is so impossibly thin that it seems to be held up – in defiance of all laws of gravity – by crazy-angled sticks, some that aren't connected to anything. 'Designing the bridge, we thought abstractly of contemporary dance and music: seeing the bridge as a convergence of art and structure leading people towards the city's art galleries.'

BUILDING THE BRIDGE

In May 2007, Baulderstone Hornibrook Queensland was selected as the preferred tenderer to design and construct the new Tank Street Bridge. In October that year, on-site construction began, with completion scheduled for late 2009: in time for the 150th-anniversary celebration's of the foundation of the State of Queensland.

On the site, the builders were confronted by the tangle of expressways that line the northern side of the river. An elegant, slim and tapered two-legged concrete pier winds up from the water as it squeezes between the River Walk and the expressway above, twisting as it rises. On the south side, a similar two-legged pier was built on a small concrete 'island' (piles sunk in the river had to be capped with a concrete island to fend off any boats on a collision course with the bridge). The narrow twisting shape of these piers adds to the impression that the bridge above is hovering in space: they read not as sturdy foundations anchoring the bridge, but as structurally inconsequential props, with the bridge deck gliding over the top of them.

The erection of the superstructure needed to be planned with utmost precision to ensure that the bridge would end up in the correct position when the thousands of prefabricated pieces (cables, masts, spars and deck beams) were bolted together.

The deflections of cable structures are notoriously difficult to accurately predict, particularly in the initial stages when the tensions in the cables are small. This is because the apparent extensions of a cable with low tension are large, whereas the apparent extensions of a highly stressed cable are small; think of how it is easy to move the end of a sagging rope by pulling, whereas pulling a taut rope generates little movement. The engineers call this non-linear behaviour.

When constructing large, complex structures, there are two basic approaches to ensure that the completed project has the correct geometry. The first is to constantly monitor the position of the structure during construction, making adjustments along the way. The second is to accurately prefabricate all the components, and then confirm by scenario planning and sophisticated analysis that connecting all the components together without adjustment will result in an acceptable final geometry. For Kurilpa Bridge, the complexity of the structure and the time available for erection meant that the builders had to take second option.

The constructors were forced to rely on the accuracy of the designers' predictions. There were no opportunities for taking up any slack in the cables or lengthening or shortening the sticks, after the components were erected. The hollow steel sticks were prefabricated to an exact length; and when erecting them, the bridge builders had to locate the top end of each at a specific point in space. The many steel cables fixed to the tops of the sticks were manufactured in the UK to precise individual lengths, and checked just prior to erection, due to the fact that they couldn't be adjusted once they were in place.

As the bridge was built, it progressively cantilevered out over the river. At each stage of this process, the engineers had to run complex structural calculations to see if the part-completed structure was behaving in accordance with computer predictions, taking into account all the supporting cables and any temporary props. The bridge deck was prefabricated in 12.8 metre segments craned into place from a barge moored in the river. Baulderstone's project manager, Paul Stathis, remembers, 'We were building the bridge piece by piece, and at times, night by night. With the exception of the bridge deck and the crossbeams [the horizontal tensegrity sticks], every element of the structure was different, in a sense, random. But the building process was definitely not speculative or random: each step was planned'.

A PEOPLE'S BRIDGE

As the bridge neared completion, the community was invited to name it, and the Tank Street Bridge became the Kurilpa Bridge (after 'Kurilpa', the Aboriginal name for the place where the bridge lands on the south side of the river). The Aboriginal people were consulted and their stories inscribed on the bridge for all to see and to remind everyone of a wider and much older Australian heritage than the State's colonial history. Queensland's 150th anniversary deadline was met and, on the 4th of October 2009 the bridge was opened by the Premier, Anna Bligh. In festive spirits, thousands of people walked across the new bridge.

At the southern end of the bridge, the ramp coils around on itself. Like a centrifuge, it launches pedestrians on their trajectory path across the bridge and into the city. Coming the other way, walkers wind down to the parkland pace of South Bank.

Early piling under the Riverside Expressway
Building the south-side (island) pier
The first section over the Riverside Expressway
The steel 'masts' being shipped in by barge

Standing on the bridge has the feeling of being in a linear outdoor room

From the South Bank side, the sweeping ramp heightens anticipation of reaching the main structure

Crossing the Kurilpa Bridge is a journey: the distance between the landing points is 470 metres. For the whole of this length there is an awning, an abstract street verandah that transforms the bridge into a linear outdoor room. Along the way there are several small 'sitting rooms' off to each side; places to stop and take in the views; contemplate the geometrics of the bridge structure; have a chat; a rest; a drink from the water bubbler.

The awning seems to float overhead. Closer inspection shows that it is suspended from the tensegrity structure. Out of sight on top of the awning are panels of solar electricity cells that power the bridge's night-time light show. In the evenings, the bridge is lit with a sophisticated LED lighting scheme that is programmed to produce an endless array of coloured lighting effects.

No matter how beautiful the bridge is at night or how convenient it is in the day, some are dismayed by the novelty of its disruptive form. It is natural for people to resist what they don't know or understand. In time, some of these critics will become used to this bridge and appreciate the fact that it is built for them, not cars, and provides a place poised above the river where people can pause and experience the pleasure of being between two realms. For most, already the bridge is a delight.

EXPERIENCING THE BRIDGE

The Kurilpa Bridge is disturbing in a positive sense. We know it to be a bridge but the spiky structure and gravity-defying thinness of the deck, make it difficult to compare this bridge with all the other bridges we are familiar with. Charles Jencks, the architectural writer, has noted people's propensity to compare an unfamiliar building or structure with something they already know. 'People invariably see one building in terms of another, or in terms of a similar object: in short, as a metaphor. The more unfamiliar the modern building is, the more they will compare it metaphorically with what they know.' So far the bridge has been compared with the masts and spars of sailing boats (a reference to the river) and with scaffolding (perhaps a connection to the city backdrop). There will be many other metaphorical connections invoked as the bridge embeds itself in the personal and collective memories of Brisbanites.

Any developed cognitive idea of the Kurilpa Bridge cannot be gained from a single encounter or a one-liner metaphor, but requires repeated encounters from many viewpoints and at different times of the day and night. This bridge transforms conventional perceptions of Brisbane, and also transforms people's experience and expectations of crossing the river.

The long thin deck with its signature spiky cloud above, is exuberant and expressive. The bridge transcends the utilitarian, to celebrate both the act of crossing the river and the city it ties together. In addition to its purely functional task of uniting the two banks, the Kurilpa Bridge is like a work of art on a very large scale. Like art, it has the power to connect us to other worlds, through seeing things in new ways.

For those who take time to pause, the bridge opens a window onto new perspectives of the familiar world around them: the city skyline, GoMA and the State Library, the flowing river, changing seasons, and the Aboriginal people who once inhabited this place, their ancient culture and their spiritual connection to Kurilpa.

This bridge transforms conventional perceptions of Brisbane, and transforms also people's experience and expectations of crossing the river.

When engineers … discuss aesthetics and architects study what cranes do, we are on the right road.

(Ove Arup, 1980)

HAIG BECK AND JACKIE COOPER

HYBRIDITY AND CHAOS

1 Suspension bridge: Golden Gate Bridge
2 Cable-stayed bridge: Hong Kong-Shenzhen Bridge
3 Arch bridge: Sydney Harbour Bridge
4 Beam bridge: Parrotts Ferry Bridge
5 Truss bridge: Pont de Quebec, the longest truss bridge in the world
6 John Roebling's Niagara Falls suspension bridge (1851–55)

For more than a century, engineers have sought 'elegant' design solutions for bridges. From the engineering perspective, elegance has been not merely a matter of utility – of limiting redundancy (that is, minimising the use of non-essential structure and structurally unnecessary material) – but also a matter of aesthetics. In the design of bridges, the aesthetic ideal is to express simply and directly the single structural system that supports a bridge deck and the live loads. (The weights of the various components of a bridge, which are constants, are termed 'dead' loads, while those variable loads due to traffic, wind and seismic activity are 'live' loads.)

In 200 years of intuition, ingenuity and invention, engineers have distilled the design of bridges into just five primary structural types: suspension (1), cable-stayed (2), arch (3), beam (4) and truss (5). (It is an interesting contradiction that engineers hold no inhibitions about requiring structural singularity in the design of bridge decks, which efficiently combine different structural systems, materials and fabrication technologies. Might this be because the structural members in bridge decks are out of sight?)

First a word about 'type': In his *Enciclopédie Méthodique, Architecture* (published in 1825), Quatremère de Quincy differentiates between 'model' and 'type'. 'The model, as understood in the practical execution of the art, is an object that should be repeated as it is; the type, on the contrary, is an object after which each [artist] can conceive works of art that may have no resemblance ...' . For example; in our minds we can imagine a suspension bridge – not any particular suspension bridge, just the idea of one – and what we imagine is a 'type'. This typological image we carry in our mind's eye, allows us to readily identify a suspension bridge when we see one. A 'type' has characteristics that all members of that type share, without any of those members looking alike.

> In 200 years of intuition, ingenuity and invention, engineers have distilled the design of bridges into just five primary structural types

The engineering urge to express typological clarity in bridge design is evidently very powerful, considering how few exceptions there are to the rule, that there be only a single structural system supporting a bridge deck, and those few exceptions relate specifically to the design of suspension bridges in the mid to late 19th-century. In 1854, Charles Ellet's Wheeling suspension bridge (1847–49) was blown down in a storm. (It was reported that during the storm the bridge was subjected to torsional movement and vertical undulations that rose almost as high as the towers.) At that time, John Roebling was nearing the completion of his Niagara Falls suspension bridge (1851–55), which had a very deep deck-stiffening truss. Roebling decided to increase deck rigidity by adding cable-stays between the trussed-deck and the adjacent cliff-face (6).

The Wheeling Bridge was rebuilt in 1860, this time incorporating a deck-stiffening truss; and in 1871 Washington Roebling (son of John) added cable-stayed elements to further brace the deck (7). Also in 1871, Rowland Mason Ordish's Albert Bridge was being built to a design based on cable-stayed principles, though with some suspension features – which were augmented, for structural reasons – in 1884 (by another engineer), giving the bridge more the character of a suspension bridge (8) than its earlier cable-stayed form. And around this time John Roebling was also working on the design for the Brooklyn Bridge (1870–83), which included cable-stayed elements to increase the rigidity of the deck (9).

In each of these examples, a hybrid structure was required to overcome structural problems, then inherent in the design of suspension bridges. Once the significance of deck stiffness was more clearly understood, this phase of structural hybridity passed. The designers of suspension bridges returned to pure suspension systems (and cable-stayed bridges were not attempted again until the 1950s, by which time their structural principles were better understood and cable technology had advanced).

KURILPA BRIDGE

The structural design report prepared by Arup for the Tank Street (Kurilpa) Bridge competition entry states that the bridge 'is based on the concept of tensegrity'. The elegant thing about tensegrity structures is that the two stresses (the pushing and pulling forces) are separated out: a member is either in pure compression or pure tension. In a tensegrity structure, islands of compression are isolated inside a continuous network of lines of tension. It is easy to identify which is which: members in tension are cable-like and very thin, and the ones in compression are stick-like and relatively thick. A genuine tensegrity structure can be easily identified by the fact that the compression members (sticks) are attached only to tension members (cables); and compression members are not directly connected to other compression members. Tensegrity structures can be light and structurally efficient but have an inherent tendency to flex and move under 'live' loads. Compared to other structural systems, they are what engineers would term very 'lively', which limits their practical application.

It is not surprising that although there are pure tensegrity elements incorporated into the final design, the bridge structure (the Arup design report notes) 'works in a similar manner to a cable-stayed bridge'. Some critics have observed that elements of the structure are reminiscent of an inverted Fink truss. This is the first disquieting fact about the bridge: not that it isn't a pure tensegrity structure, but that it is a *hybrid* structure – anathema to an engineering aesthetic.

The engineers used pure tensegrity elements (in this case, suspended horizontal spars) to laterally brace the Kurilpa Bridge's array of masts and to support the awning (10), and a stiffer and more conventional mast and cable arrangement for the primary support of the bridge deck (11). Yet even here, the engineering solution is not conventional. Most cable-stayed bridges use a single or pair of pylons at one or both ends of a span. The Kurilpa Bridge pylons consist of two pairs of oddly-angled masts at each end of the main span. Unlike other cable-stayed designs, these 'mast-like' pylons are not rigidly fixed to the piers below. They are pinned – at one end, to the southern pier, and at the other, to the bridge deck structure at the point where the deck slides over the northern pier.

Pinning the masts at their lower end allows them to swivel, and – being attached to tension cables at the other end – to absorb minute movements in the tension cables as the bridge is subject to 'live' loads from foot traffic and gusts of wind. Permitting one end of the bridge deck to 'slide', allows for thermal expansion and contraction. (The sliding action is constrained by bearings fixed under the deck to the pier, so that movement is only horizontally along the line of the span.)

In a tensegrity structure, islands of compression are isolated inside a continuous network of lines of tension.

7 Charles Ellet's Wheeling suspension bridge (built 1847, rebuilt in 1860 and strengthened in 1871)

8 Rowland Mason Ordish's Albert Bridge (1871, with suspension features added in 1884)

9 John Roebling's Brooklyn Bridge (1870–83)

10 Kurilpa Bridge: Pure tensegrity structure

11 Kurilpa Bridge: Primary mast and cable-stayed structure

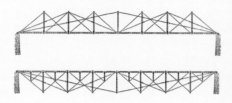

12 Kurilpa Bridge: Secondary mast structure
13 Fink truss and the same truss inverted for comparison with the Kurilpa Bridge structure

On each side of the bridge deck there is also a series of secondary masts. These compression members are pinned at their lower end to the edge of the bridge deck structure; with tension cables running from the tops back to the deck at the centre point between the adjacent pairs of secondary masts, to provide additional support to the deck (12). This system of secondary masts and their cables form what superficially appears to be a version of an inverted Fink truss (13). (And the engineer's earlier concept diagram for this secondary support structure, closely approximates such a truss.) The structural system of secondary masts and cables acts in concert with the primary 'cable-stayed' system to form a truss. One can trace the path of the cable-stays from the tops of the primary support masts (located over the piers), down to the bottom of these secondary masts.

The deck support structure relies on the interaction of the three distinct structural systems: the cluster of masts over the piers and their cable-stays that provide the primary support; the truss system these cable-stays form in conjunction with the secondary masts, supplying additional deck support; and the tensegrity spars that provide the lateral bracing. All three systems are integrated into a structural whole, in which all the masts (and spars) are subject to compressive (pushing) forces, and all the cables to tensile (pulling) forces. The concept of tensegrity is manifested above the bridge deck in the clear separation of the compression and tension elements.

HYBRIDITY VS ELEGANCE

For much of the last century, a powerful taboo operated to prevent engineers from using hybrid structures as the primary support system for bridge decks. Such a taboo (more accurately, negative heuristics) is used by professionals to guide practice and so avoid technical pitfalls. Bridge design has been for a long time a far from precise science and a practice periodically subject to catastrophic failures; the incalculable complexities introduced by structural hybridity, only increased the risk of design failure. Put simply, historically, engineers learned that doing the calculations for a single structural system was difficult enough without introducing further complications.

In a non-linear hybrid structure like the Kurilpa Bridge, stasis is achieved through the combined interaction of several hundred individual structural members: some in compression, many more in tension, each occupying different spatial co-ordinates and subject to different stresses generated by the 'dead' loads and the constantly changing stresses of variable 'live' loads. Even a slight variation in the length or angle of a single member will affect all the others, and (potentially) the structural and functional integrity of the whole. Like Edward Lorenz's 'flap of a butterfly's wings in Brazil', a small change can lead to a ripple effect through the whole system, with unpredictable outcomes.

The designers of the Kurilpa Bridge could identify these potential problems in advance because they used powerful computers able to swiftly model the structural and spatial implications of any change to the design (14). Such analysis requiring difficult mathematical calculations was not possible before the recent advent of very fast computers with huge computational power and the development of sophisticated three-dimensional structural modelling software. These advances

Bridge design has been for a long time a far from precise science and a practice potentially subject to catastrophic failures . . .

25

in computing have made the accurate prediction of the behaviour of complex structural systems possible for the first time in engineering history.

Computers have helped release engineers from the taboo against hybridity. However, typically such taboos have cultural, as well as, practical dimensions and are the result of social custom and even emotional aversion. The engineer's aversion to hybridity and the quest for elegant, simple design may spring from concerns far more profound than avoiding the problems of complicated maths. There are powerful and deep-seated cultural injunctions against the hybrid: it is a mongrel, a bastard, impure. The distinction between pure and impure – between good and evil – is fundamental in all religions and philosophies. And long before the rise of religions, the distinction between pure and impure was a survival strategy hardwired into humans from the time of their earliest sentient experiences.

The primordial struggle between good and evil is evident also in the human instinct to resist entropy and bring things to order. Bringing an order to things is something we all do, to such a degree that ordering might best describe the human condition. The will to order has an aesthetic dimension. Mathematicians and scientists speak of 'elegant' equations (as in: $E=mc^2$, possibly the most elegant equation of all). There is an emotive correspondence between 'order' and 'elegance' that we all recognise: that satisfying condition of neatness, ingenious simplicity and precision. Designers intuitively recognise an elegant solution to a particular problem when it manifests these qualities, and they actively seek such solutions. Edsger W Dijkstra, one of the greats of modern mathematics, has noted that there is a practical dimension to elegant solutions: 'Simplicity is the prerequisite for reliability'.

> There are powerful and deep seated cultural injunctions against the hybrid: it is a mongrel, a bastard, impure

14 Computer design modelling of the Kurilpa Bridge structure
15 Isambard Kingdom Brunel's Clifton Suspension Bridge (designed 1830, built 1862–64)
16 Leon Moisseiff's Tacoma Narrows Bridge collapses (1940)

Engineers engaged in the design of bridges have subscribed to the dictum of elegance; not only for practical reasons of safety and economy, but also because they too are subject to the universally shared and inescapable, visceral desire for order.

Engineers are also subject to the fashionable notions of beauty of their day. The great British engineer, Isambard Kingdom Brunel, remarked to his brother after presenting his design for the Clifton Suspension Bridge (designed in 1830) (15): 'Of all the wonderful feats I have performed … I think yesterday I performed the most wonderful. I produced unanimity among 15 men who were all quarrelling about that most ticklish subject – taste'.

Within the fraternity of bridge designers, engineers have their own notions of what constitutes beauty. Leon Moisseiff, one of the designers of San Francisco's Golden Gate Bridge, called his Tacoma Narrows design – with its elegant, super-thin road deck – 'the most beautiful bridge in the world' (ironically, this was just before its spectacular collapse in 1940) (16). And when engineers from around the world were polled recently, they selected Robert Maillart's Salginatobel Bridge in Switzerland (1929–30) as 'the most beautiful bridge of the twentieth century' (17). Maillart achieved what his American contemporary, Moisseiff (both were born in 1872), aspired to: bridge designs that express the structure with absolute aesthetic clarity, while using the bare minimum of material. In this respect they were both following the Functionalist aesthetic diktat of their day.

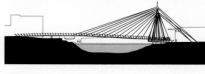

17 Robert Maillart's Salginatobel Bridge (1929–30)

18 Kurilpa Bridge: Preliminary design for a cable-stayed structure with a mast on the north side of the river

19 Kurilpa Bridge: Preliminary design for a cable-stayed structure with a mast on the south side of the river

20 Kurilpa Bridge: Preliminary design for an arch structure with the deck suspended below it

21 Kurilpa Bridge: Preliminary design for a suspension bridge structure

22 Kurilpa Bridge: Preliminary design for a truss structure

23 Gallery of Modern Art

EUREKA!

The will to order is particularly strong in designers. They share a developed desire to arrange, classify and constrain in order to reach the essence of a problem and be well positioned to solve it. To arrive at a solution, designers occasionally experience – Eureka! – moments of creative inspiration; but they also know that most design is hard work that requires a continuing and gruelling process of refinement. And so it appears to have been in the design of the Kurilpa Bridge.

Conflicting criteria had to be satisfied, some arising from functional limitations, but others of the designers' making. River navigation required the underside of the bridge deck to be 11 metres above high water for nearly the full width of the river. On the high-set, northern side, this presented no great problem, but on the much lower, southern side, it meant that a very long ramp was needed. Keeping the ramp length to a minimum would facilitate pedestrian access and reduce impact on the little riverside park the bridge was to land in. There were also contextual urban design issues: fitting the bridge into a neighbourhood with high-rise office towers on one side of the river and low-set, civic buildings on the other. In addition, the competition brief required a bridge that would be a 'landmark statement' that possessed the 'wow' factor.

The designers preferred a bridge with a low silhouette that would not overshadow the adjacent low-set Gallery of Modern Art

From the perspective of a structural purist, several bridge typologies would each individually provide the necessary clearance and shallow bridge deck that a shorter ramp required: a 'cable-stayed' structure with a pylon on one side of the river (18) or the other (19); an arch with the deck suspended below it (20); a suspension bridge (21); or a truss structure (22). Detailed designs were prepared for each, but all were rejected on aesthetic grounds.

The designers preferred a bridge with a low silhouette that would not overshadow the adjacent low-set Gallery of Modern Art (23). The 'cable-stayed' design, with its tall pylon on the north side of the river, avoids this conflict. But the long axis of these different bridge typologies with their ramped approaches, appear to have been problematic to the designers. There was no difficulty on the northern side of the river, where the trajectory of the bridge is an extension of the Tank Street axis: the street, the ramped approach and the bridge deck are all part of the same linear continuum. However, on the south side, this axial trajectory is disrupted: the ramp from the bridge deck must turn back on itself in order to arrive at the public walkway that skirts the river. From the perspective of a traffic engineer, this may not have been a problem, but aesthetically it truncates the graceful lines traced by the decks of these bridges.

The 'cable-stayed' bridge with a raked-pylon at the south-side of the river was excluded from contention because it towered above the Gallery. Still, the manner in which the ramp might be elegantly coiled around the base of the pylon seemed to offer a way out of the ramp impasse, if only the pylon wasn't so high. The designers were also troubled by the raked-pylon, 'cable-stayed' solution because it had been used so many times already and in far more dramatic settings: to do it again here, would hardly make this design a 'landmark statement'. It was at this point, they remember, that they found themselves at a standstill.

And then Tristram Carfrae, the lead design engineer from Arup, said 'How about a tensegrity bridge'? The suggestion was not wholly serious: Carfrae well understood the inappropriateness of 'lively' tensegrity structures to bridge design. On his part, it may have been little more than a ploy worthy of his hero, Buckminster Fuller, to free up their thinking. (As a young graduate, Carfrae spent time in Arup's lightweight structures laboratory in London, where he heard Buckminster Fuller, the American engineer and futurist, speak. As with many who met Fuller, it was an inspirational encounter that shaped Carfrae's thinking about structures and sustainability. Among Fuller's many inventions, one stands out in the design community's consciousness: his geodesic domes based on the structural principles of tensegrity.) (24)

Michael Rayner, the lead architect on the team (who was uncontaminated by engineering taboos), took Carfrae literally and looked at tensegrity structures – particularly the sculptures designed by Kenneth Snelson (25) – and thought 'Why not'? Rayner made some rough sketches for a tensegrity bridge (26) which got Carfrae thinking seriously about his tensegrity proposition. The resulting first 'tensegrity' design ticked all the boxes: low silhouette, very thin deck, a coiled ramp that worked aesthetically, and plenty of 'wow!'.

The Kurilpa Bridge is typologically based on hybridity, which is disquieting to purists.

CREATIVE CHAOS

Regarding ideas about beauty, many contemporary bridge designers remain constrained by the anti-hybrid taboo, and are guided by the aesthetics of Functionalist Modernism, which calls for elegant simplicity and structural clarity. The Kurilpa Bridge is typologically based on hybridity, which is disquieting to purists. However, from a functionalist's viewpoint, advances in computer design and programming raise a question: Does hybridity really matter anymore?

Another disquieting aspect of the bridge, is that superficially, it appears structurally incomprehensible. The structural system that supports the bridge deck is not expressed simply and directly, and does not reassuringly present the span to spectators, as stable and secure. The designers have eschewed the universally accepted paradigm of structural purity to produce a structurally improbable array of angled masts and cables. Even more disquieting is that although we are informed that the masts and cables support the bridge deck, they give every appearance of not doing so: instead, it's as if they are supported by the impossibly thin deck.

Arup's early structural design established the bridge structure in principle: an integrated system of pinned, 'cable-stayed' masts over the piers to support the bridge deck; a secondary 'minor' deck support system, comprising of masts and cables in a Fink truss-like configuration; and a pure tensegrity system of spars and cables to aid the lateral stability of the whole (10–12). There is a diagram called 'the simple concept' showing these separate structural elements integrated into a single system (27). This structure was refined into what became the final built form through a tactic the designers call 'creative chaos' (28, 29).

'Creative chaos' is artistic licence by another name. Changes to the angles of the masts and slight adjustments to their location along the deck edge were done by the architects by eye. Their objective was to make the disposition of the masts and spars

24 Buckminster Fuller and geodesic dome
25 Kenneth Snelson, Easy-K (1970)
Aluminium and stainless steel, 6.5 x 6.5 x 32m
Exhibition, Sonsbeek '70, Arnhem, Holland
26 Early tensegrity bridge sketch by Michael Rayner

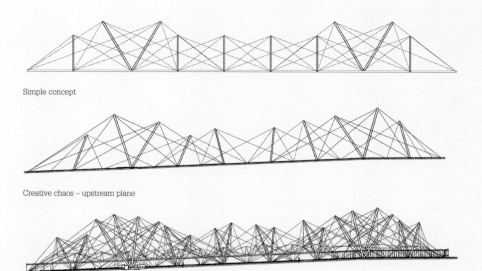

Simple concept

Creative chaos – upstream plane

Creative chaos

27 Kurilpa Bridge: Structural system simple concept
28 Kurilpa Bridge: Creative chaos – upstream plane
29 Kurilpa Bridge: Creative chaos

appear purely random, defeating any attempt by spectators to find a clear structural order to the bridge design. The engineers were complicit in the aestheticisation of the structural design. They advised the architects on the viability of their interventions at each stage of this process of creative chaos refinement, and then subjected the finalised design to full mathematical analysis (a complex task that had to be undertaken in London every time the design for the bridge was changed).

As a design tactic, 'creative chaos' was a highly empirical operation, yet still subject to the complex integrated structural logic of the bridge as a whole. Michael Rayner remembers attempting minor modifications to the angles of the main masts at a late stage in the design process, to 'make them appear even more random'. When the revised design was run through the computers in London, these small changes produced unexpected and unwanted results: other masts and some spars shifted position to such an extent that they became major obstructions to the free movement of pedestrians across the bridge. Such dramatic and unexpected results from a small change in a complex system might also serve as a controlled demonstration of Chaos Theory in operation.

(It should be remembered here that there are differing ideas about the nature of chaos. The ancient Greeks conceived of chaos, 'x', as a formless void filled with darkness; and the Greek world was created harmoniously out of this chaos, such that there was order in diversity. Contemporary Chaos Theory is a scientific hypothesis that proposes that apparently random phenomena have an underlying order: that complex natural systems obey rules, but are so sensitive, that small initial changes can cause unexpected final results, giving an impression of randomness.)

Such dramatic and unexpected results from a small change in a complex system might also serve as a controlled demonstration of Chaos Theory in operation.

A strange game is being played here by the designers: instead of creating order – an object of all design – they actively attempt to subvert it. The nearest architectural equivalent is Deconstruction: an architectural style fashionable among the post-modern avant-garde in the 1980s and 90s. Buildings that exhibit the many deconstructivist styles are characterised formally by fragmentation and non-orthogonal geometry to give an appearance of controlled chaos (30). Deconstruction (the architectural style, not the French literary theory) stands in opposition to the ordered rationality of Modernism. As with all avant-garde cultural movements, it is iconoclastic in purpose and practice, seeking to challenge and overturn traditional beliefs, customs and values.

As the designers no doubt intended, the deconstruction of the Kurilpa Bridge structure (31) will disrupt most people's preconceptions of what a bridge is. The design – whether disturbingly crazy, as it will be for some, or a little magical, as it is to many others – shifts this bridge out of the realm of the purely functional and utilitarian, into the poetical. No-one who encounters the Kurilpa Bridge can cross it without momentarily viewing through new eyes the river it spans and the two sides of the city it joins.

The hybrid nature of the Kurilpa Bridge structure might offend some conservative engineering sensibilities. However, there will be many who find themselves engagingly perplexed by the whimsical display of structural anarchy. At that moment, they may wish to reflect on an observation of Isaac Asimov: 'The most exciting phrase to hear in science, the one that heralds new discoveries, is not 'Eureka!', but 'That's funny'.

30 Coop Himmelb(l)au's 'Deconstructivist' Akron Museum of Art, Pittsburgh

31 Kurilpa Bridge

A strange game is being played here by the designers: instead of creating order – an object of all design – they actively attempt to subvert it.

'… the proper management of materials and of site, as well as a thrifty balancing of costs and common sense in the construction of works'.

(Roman architect-engineer, Marcus Vitruvius Pollio, first century BC)

HAIG BECK AND JACKIE COOPER

BRIDGE ART

When not campaigning, and given the necessary time and opportunity, Roman military engineers were prodigious builders. They linked entire regions with arrow-straight, permanent paved roads, built soaring multi-tiered masonry aqueducts and massive stone-arched bridges. So well engineered were these bridges and so robustly constructed that many have survived the vicissitude of 2000 years of storms, floods and wars. They exhibit a straightforward elegance that we still admire: they are functional and unadorned by superfluous ornamentation. Every stone is structurally essential. Joints align to exhibit inherent stresses and resistance. Primary and secondary members are distinguished in the way the respective masonry surfaces are dressed: usually rugged at the base where the forces are greatest, and refined where constructional precision is required and at points of human contact.

The core structure of the Pons Fabricius (1) in the heart of Rome (62BC) is built from roughly finished tuff, a soft greyish volcanic rock. The wedge-shaped voussoirs forming the arches are precisely dressed in a contrasting white and slightly harder travertine. Both stones were locally quarried and easily worked.

The builders of the Alcántarra Bridge (AD106) erected far from Rome in the isolated vastness of central Spain (2), had access only to a single stone: the local granite (hard and difficult to work). Here the builders dressed the granite differently to contrast the primary and secondary elements of the bridge structure: the abutments, piers, and the core structure are rough-hewn, while the voussoirs are so finely shaped and exactly fitted by the masons, as to require no mortar in the joints between them.

An expressive and elegant beauty – an engineering aesthetic – characterises all Roman bridges. This aesthetic arises from the economy of means that minimises redundancy and relies on minimally worked, locally quarried stone. At some time in the first century BC, the Roman architect-engineer, Marcus Vitruvius Pollio set out in the second chapter of his treatise, *Ten Books of Architecture*, nine fundamental principles of architecture: two related to economy, which he defined as: '… the proper management of materials and of site, as well as a thrifty balancing of costs and common sense in the construction of works'.

The link between economy of means and notions of beauty led to one of the most spectacular engineering failures of the 20th century.

Historically, this correlation between economy of means and an engineering aesthetic is nowhere more pronounced than in the brilliant achievements of the Gothic master builders in dematerialising massive masonry walls of cathedrals and elevating ponderous stone spires heavenwards (3). This same ethos of economy of materials, is also evident in the engineering structures of the Industrial Revolution; grounded in a desire for economic efficiency. Engineers were anxious to achieve the most favourable power-to-weight ratios and to resist stresses with the least amount of material: in short, to ensure nothing was redundant. This concern is cogently illustrated in the evolution of the early iron bridges: the Iron Bridge – the very first iron bridge, completed in 1781 (4) – used 378 tons of iron to span 30 metres. Just a few years later, in 1796, the Wearmouth Bridge, only the third iron bridge in the world, required slightly less than 285 tons of iron to span 75 metres (5).

The link between economy of means and notions of beauty led to one of the most spectacular engineering failures of the 20th century. The Tacoma Narrows Bridge was a suspension bridge with an elegant, slender deck-to-span ratio 1:350. Its designer, Leon Moisseiff, called this 'the most beautiful bridge in the world'. However, his design proved too slender, too economical in its use of materials: the bridge collapsed shortly after it was opened in 1940 (6).

1 Pons Fabricius, Rome, Italy (62BC)
2 Alcantara Bridge, Cáceres Province, Spain (103–06AD)
3 Strasbourg Cathedral, France (1176–1439)
4 Thomas Pritchard and Abraham Darby III: Iron Bridge, Coalbrookdale, England (1778–81)

Threaded through a freeway tangle on one side of the Brisbane River and constrained by height limitations on the other, the Kurilpa Bridge necessitated Vitruvius's time-honoured formula of '… the proper management of materials and of site, as well as a thrifty balancing of costs and common sense in the construction of works'. The brief additionally stipulated an 'icon', experientially exciting and visually memorable. In meeting this range of demands, the designers opted for an extreme, lightweight structural solution, a radical 'tensegrity-like' structure, using a minimum of material to span the river (7).

Reflecting on the design of Kurilpa Bridge, Tristram Carfrae, Arup's lead design engineer on the project, remembers as a graduate trainee in Arup's lightweight structures laboratory in London being influenced by a talk given by the American engineer and futurist, R Buckminster Fuller (8). 'I remember him saying "use less material, just use less" – a great approach to life. This has become fundamental to my thinking about structure and sustainability: to use less and make more of it.'

ZEITGEIST

The modern idea of zeitgeist discloses how the artefacts of a people express the intellectual, moral and cultural climate of their era. Thus we observe in Roman buildings and bridges evidence of aesthetic and political values, as well as, the obvious functional purposes of these structures. Whereas Roman bridges were primarily utilitarian spans intended to speed communications and regulate colonised populations; they transcended mundane use. Like Roman palaces and temples, bridges built by Romans served to express Roman power and authority: Rome's subjugation not only of regions and people, but also of nature itself.

> 'I remember him saying "use less material, just use less" – a great approach to life. This has become fundamental to my thinking about structure and sustainability: to use less and make more of it'.

Zeitgeist as a notion was propounded in the early 19th-century by the German Romantics. This transformational idea proposed that works of art, and indeed artefacts such as buildings and monuments, are open to interpretation. Interpretations vary according to the viewer and the moment, and they can shift and alter according to changes in values and perception. Since the Renaissance, the subjects of art have been perceived as allegorical, and those interested in appreciating fine art have looked behind and beyond the surface image of paintings and sculpture for allegorical meaning. Consider Botticelli's 'Birth of Venus' (c1486) (9). Ernst Gombrich deemed the work to suggest a neoplatonic reading in keeping with the Florentine Platonic Academy of the time Botticelli painted the work: viewers observing Venus, the most beautiful of the goddesses, might initially experience a physical response which then lifted their minds towards the Creator. The gaze of an atheistic 21st-century viewer is less likely to be transported to a moral realm of existential reflection, but to remain fixated on the decorative beauty of the subject and the artist's superb technique, informed by a distanced awareness of allegorical meaning (and no doubt also by the painting's aura of celebrity). So, interpretations of art vary according to who is viewing and the values through which they focus – both personal values and those of the prevailing zeitgeist.

5 First Wearmouth Bridge, Sunderland, England (1796)

6 Leon Moisseiff's Tacoma Narrows Bridge, Washington State, USA (1937–40)

7 Kurilpa Bridge under construction

8 R Buckminster Fuller describing the engineering of one of his geodesic dome structures

The George Washington Bridge in New York (1927–31) illustrates the way that bridges might distill the zeitgeist. To support the suspension cables while this bridge was under construction, steel towers with a tracery of crisscross bracing were erected. The designers intended to encase these steel structures in concrete to form monumental pylons at each end of the span, and then clad the pylons in granite detailed in the Classical manner. However, that was before public consciousness intervened.

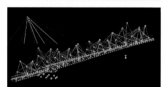

9 Sandro Botticelli's 'Birth of Venus' (c1486)

10 George Washington Bridge, New York, USA (1927–31)

11 Arup's application of three-dimensional structural modelling software to the structural design of Kurilpa Bridge

Overtly 'technological' and with its chaotic, interconnected indeterminacy, this bridge is both a product and a metaphor of the digital zeitgeist.

While the bridge was still under construction, these 'provisional' steel towers were widely perceived as expressions of the streamlined, stripped, abstracted aesthetic of Functionalist Modernism that was sweeping America. It was an aesthetic that exactly matched the new 20th-century mood of the nation. Anachronistic Classical masonry was superfluous. The steel bracing was left exposed (10).

What does the Kurilpa Bridge tell us about our times? In what way is it an expression of the present zeitgeist?

In our prefatory remarks we identified a defining image of the bridge: 'To our untutored eyes, the structure supporting the Kurilpa Bridge didn't make sense: the seemingly chaotic array of cables and spiky, 'stick-like' masts and the incredible thinness of its central span, defied any structural logic we were familiar with. This bridge was contrary to our expectations'. The structural complexity of the bridge's 'tensegrity-like' form is such, that only very fast super computers running complex three-dimensional structural modelling software could accurately analyse and calculate the forces and stresses in play (11). The Kurilpa Bridge is the product of the digital age.

The use of computers, mobile phones, digital cameras and other digital technology is globally pervasive among individuals, as well as, businesses, industries and governments. A disturbing difference between the digital age and all previous periods of human development, from the stone age on, is our total dependence now on tools that we cannot make (on the forest floor, in a backyard shed or anywhere else, for that matter) and on technologies we have no hope of comprehending. We rely on digital tools and technologies for nearly every convenience and every emergency, and we do so with unquestioning faith.

Kurilpa Bridge epitomises this facet of the digital age. It is the product of the times (it would have been impossible to design or build the bridge without digital technology) and we use the bridge in utter confidence, yet without any idea as to how it stands up. Overtly 'technological' and with its chaotic, interconnected indeterminacy, this bridge is both a product and a metaphor of the digital zeitgeist.

ART

Kurilpa Bridge is a work formed not just by purely functional concerns, but also through the agency and interaction of two interdependent aesthetic systems. The minimalist engineers' aesthetic is one system: this conscious design tactic raises economy of means to an aesthetic order by stripping redundancy from the design, paring elements to their slightest profile and visually clarifying the order and particular nature of the parts. There are additionally the effects of a form-making tactic the designers refer to as 'creative chaos'. This is a kind of artistic licence, as we observe elsewhere: 'Changes to the angles of the masts and slight adjustments to their location along the deck edge were done by the architects by eye. Their objective was to make the disposition of the masts and spars appear purely random, defeating any attempt by spectators to find a clear structural order to the bridge design.'

The Kurilpa Bridge exhibits aesthetic characteristics shared with what are conventionally considered works of art, but its fundamental raison d'être – to be a bridge – raises a question: can it be considered 'art'?

The problematic question of what is art, broke through public consciousness in 1917 when Marcel Duchamp (1887–1968) tried to exhibit one of his Readymades, a work he titled 'Fountain' (12). Readymades were found objects that Duchamp chose and presented as art. His idea was to question both the adoration of art and the very notion of 'art'. 'Fountain', a urinal signed with the pseudonym 'R. Mutt', shocked the art world. When Duchamp attempted to exhibit it, the committee of the avant-garde Society of Independent Artists rejected the work, insisting it was not art. In 2004, 500 leading artists and art historians from around the world voted 'Fountain' 'the most influential art work of the 20th century'.

For a handy, omnibus definition of 'art', we can do worse than borrow from Wikipedia: 'Art is something that stimulates an individual's thoughts, emotions, beliefs, or ideas through the senses. It is also an expression of an idea and it can take many different forms and serve many different purposes. … The first and broadest sense of 'art', is the one that has remained closest to the older Latin meaning, which roughly translates to 'skill' or 'craft.'… The second and more recent sense of the word 'art', is as an abbreviation for 'creative art' or 'fine art'. … If the skill is being used in a commercial or industrial way [as in 'design'], it will be considered … 'applied art'. … Some art followers have argued that the difference between 'fine art' and 'applied art' has more to do with value judgments made about the 'art' than any clear definitional difference.'

Definitions of what is and what isn't 'art' are tricky. Values shift, and today's 'fine art' was in many cases possibly yesterday's 'applied art'. In the 21st-century it is easy to lose sight of the reality that the greatest artists of the Renaissance and Baroque, Michelangelo and Caravaggio, were in effect the Mad Men of their day, propagandists paid to promote the church and the nobility. Of course, they were formidable painters, formidable visionaries, formidable artists whose eminence has survived through the centuries. Yet in the 'pre-photography' era they occupied, when it was their technical services that were commissioned, and also at a time when the notion of the 'artist' was undivided from the classification of 'artisan', masters were rarely raised above the common ruck of workers who stood below nobles and gentle society.

In the future, who will be recognised as the substantive artists of the early digital age? Film-makers? Architects? Designers of bridges?

12 Marcel Duchamp's 'Fountain' (1917)
13 Andy Warhol's 'Campbell's Soup 1' (1968)

LAND ART

In the 1960s, Duchamp's Readymades found an exponent in Andy Warhol (who, incidentally, trained and first worked as a commercial artist). In 1962, Warhol produced silkscreen-cum-paintings of tins of Campbell's soup, and in 1968 even signed – and then sold as 'art' – actual tins of Campbell's soup. Warhol's 'Campbell's Soup 1' (1968) (13) became emblematic of 'American Pop art'.

'Pop art' generally looked to consumer society for its subject matter, removing objects from their contexts or locating them in unexpected juxtapositions. The effect was ironic and often intellectually disruptive (and in this respect reveals a connection back to Duchamp and his fellow dadaists and surrealists, as well as, forwards to the subsequent 'conceptual art' movement). Pop artists questioned the subjects of art, and also – through the use of mechanical reproduction techniques and the production of 'multiples' – notions of originality and authenticity that went to the heart of what is considered art.

A contemporary, parallel and equally questioning art movement to emerge in the late 1960s is 'land art'. 'Land art' (usually) is very large. It imposes objects or inscribes marks on the land, some discernible from space. 'Land' artists removed art

14 Walter De Maria's 'The Lightning Field', New Mexico, USA (1977)

15 Robert Smithson's 'Spiral Jetty', Utah, USA (1970)

… 'land art' is made to be experienced in the field, taking in the variability of weather and the passage of time.

from the gallery, freeing it from the scale and media imposed by the traditional salon. London's Tate Gallery describes this art movement: '"Land art" … can be seen as part of the wider Conceptual art movement in the 1960s and 1970s. "Land" artists began working directly in the landscape, sculpting it into earthworks or making structures with rocks or twigs. Some of them used mechanical earth-moving equipment …' Landscape and art work become fused visually and experientially.

Despite being photographed and exhibited on gallery walls, 'land art' is made to be experienced in the field, taking in the variability of weather and the passage of time. Walter de Maria's 'The Lightning Field' (1977) (14) is well-known and widely visited despite its isolation in a remote area of the high desert of western New Mexico. It consists of 400 polished stainless steel poles located in a grid array; the poles – 2 inches in diameter and averaging over 20 feet in height – are spaced 220 feet apart, their solid pointed tips defining a horizontal plane. This is sculpture to be walked in as much as viewed from outside. It is also intended to be experienced over extended time. Visitors book into a lodge next to the site in order to experience the work at sunset and sunrise, with or without lightning, which is not essential to appreciate the work.

The ordered regiment of polished poles set against the rugged desert horizon strikes a deep chord in many. One visitor ponders, 'Here is high tech in the middle of nowhere. This sign of human ingenuity is imposed on the wild life and stunted vegetation of the high mesa. What does it all mean?'

Often meaning in 'art' consists in awareness of the fact of one's own existence (and mortality), heightened appreciation of connectedness, or isolation too perhaps, that we at times derive from experiences associated with nature, art, literature, theatre, religion, music, architecture – or maybe crossing a bridge. Meaning does not have to arrive as an epiphany. Often it is through simple experiential moments of unconscious awareness and revelation.

BRIDGE AS ART?

The Kurilpa Bridge, at nearly half a kilometre long, is comparable in scale with 'land art'; it is experienced spatially, over time, and also aesthetically. This bridge shares qualities of 'land art' such as Walter de Maria's 'The Lightning Field' and Robert Smithson's 460 metre 'Spiral Jetty' (1970) (15). Like 'The Lightning Field', Kurilpa Bridge has a futuristic array of high-tech masts that command attention and provoke interpretation: what do they mean? Like 'Spiral Jetty', which curls up out of a lake, massive and mysterious, the bridge has a poetic relationship to water: it floats above the river as though weightless, defying logic, provoking wonderment and a frisson of pleasurable angst as one embarks on a crossing.

But a bridge does not qualify to be a 'work of art'. It is purposeful, utilitarian, an artefact designed with function, safety and durability uppermost. Art, in contrast, cannot easily be explained rationally: it exists on its own terms, free from use or purpose.

Yet even the simplest, plainest and least expressive of bridges can't help themselves. Bridges are, inherently, expressive objects. A bridge launches itself from a bank or precipice in a direct arc and lands on the opposite side. Its very form is dynamic, communicating through form the movement of travel across it, the act of uniting disconnected places. Crossing a bridge is always an act of faith requiring some degree of daring. The function of a bridge, to tie together two divided realms, also has metaphoric and even mystical connotations that no one crossing a bridge fails to register, however faintly or subliminally.

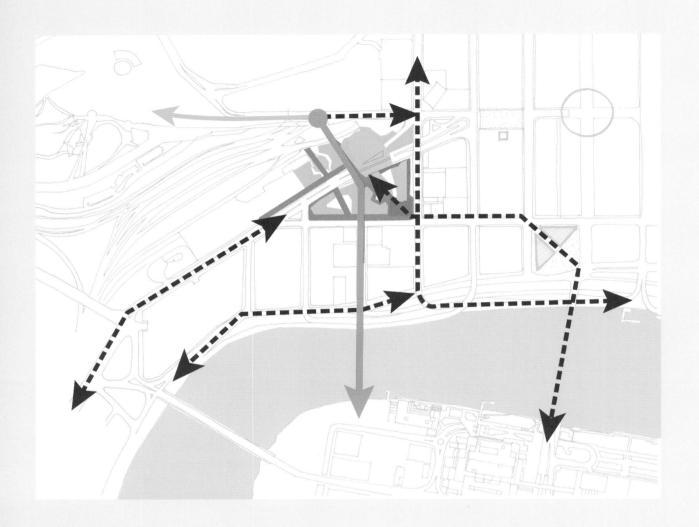

1999 planning diagram by Cox Rayner Architects
envisaging a river crossing at the Kurilpa location
Early conceptual sketch by Michael Rayner

Kenneth Snelson at work,
Easy-K (1970)
Aluminum and stainless steel
6.5 x 6.5 x 32m
Exhibition, Sonsbeek '70, Arnhem, Holland

Kurilpa Bridge's mast, strut and cable structure with the tensegrity
structure that supports the canopy suspended inside.

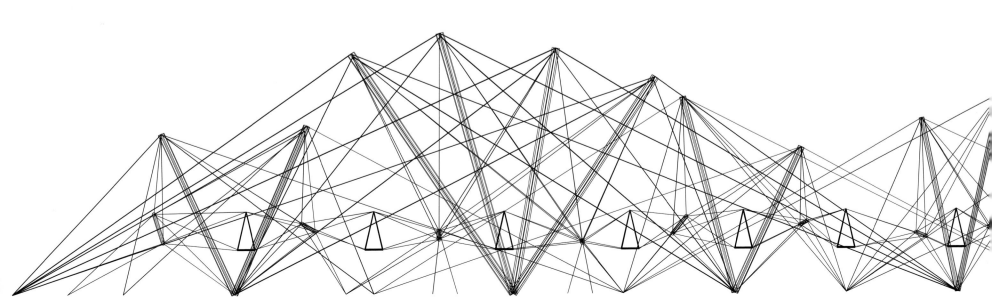

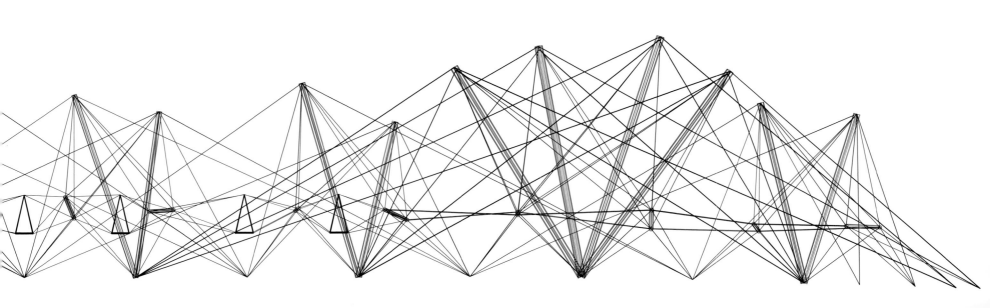

Detail of masts and cables prior to the roof canopy being installed

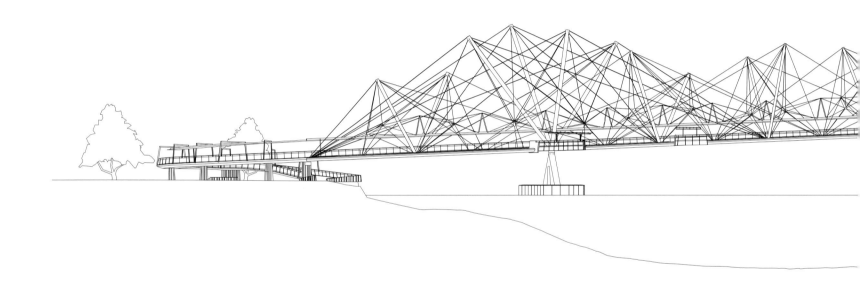

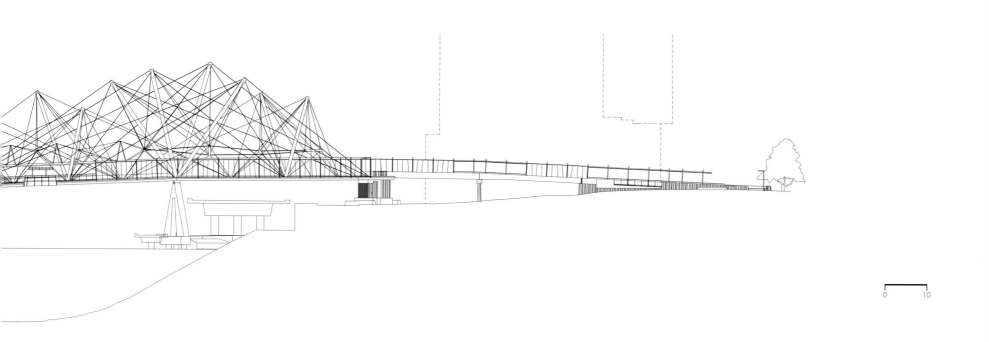

Elevation of Kurilpa Bridge from the Victoria Bridge side

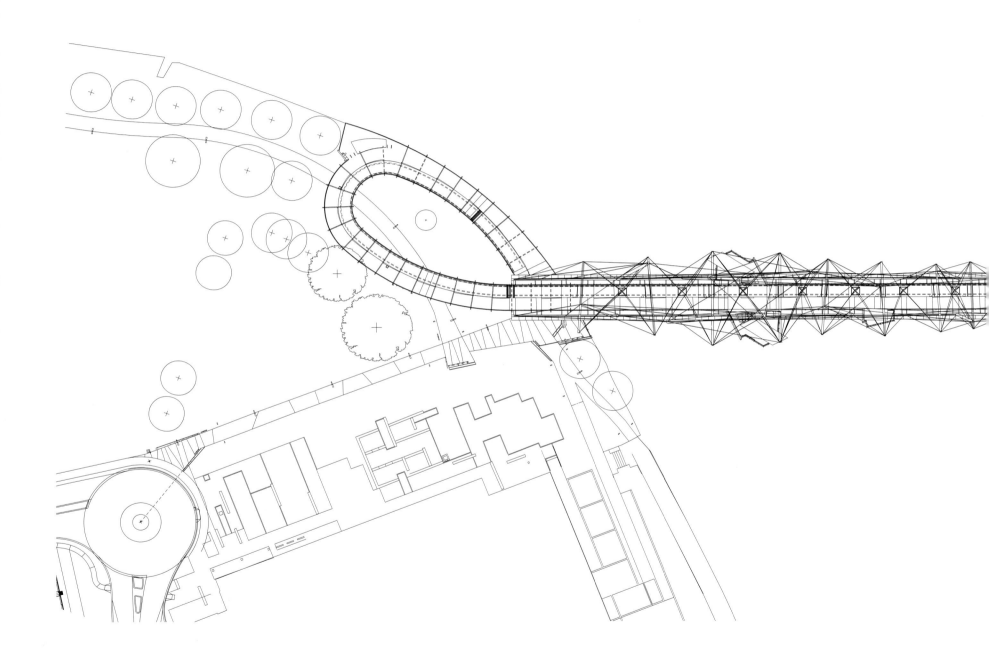

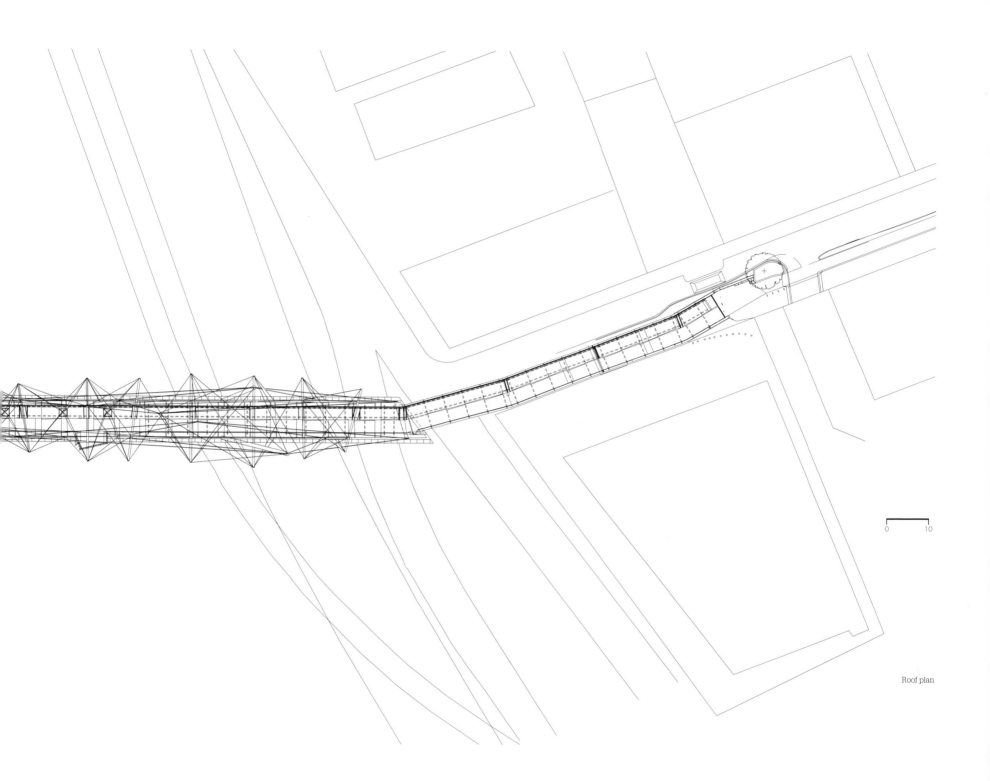

Roof plan

The masts being temporarily supported by struts
during construction

With the help of temporary struts, the structure was able to cantilever some 50 metres out over the river during the construction

One of the great challenges was to span over the Riverside Expressway, Brisbane's busiest thoroughfare, without interrupting its operation

Cyclists under the bridge on the Kurilpa Park side

Crossing from the city toward the Gallery of Modern Art
(left) and William Jolly Bridge (right)

Cyclists approaching and crossing the Bridge
The bridge as experienced by traffic on the Riverside Expressway

Kurilpa Bridge is meant to be more than a crossing and
feel like a series of linked outdoor rooms

A story told to Aboriginal children by their Elders is that a serpent created the river, ca... salt water creatures and the animals on the land. As the serpent meandered through the country... og and the sand goanna. These animals now form mountains which you can see from the Kurilpa Br...

Jagera People

The multiple cable connections to the deck often resulted in interesting forms in themselves
The Jagera People and Turrbal People contributed stories which are located along the journey

A story told to Aboriginal children by their Elders is that a serpent created the river, causing conflicts between the salt water creatures and the animals on the land. As the serpent meandered through the countryside, it also battled the green frog and the sand goanna. These animals now form mountains which you can see from the Kurilpa Bridge.

Jagera People

The sense of the bridge feeling like a linear outdoor room

A view from the Gallery of Modern Art with the two river piers
illuminated by sunlight

View over Kurilpa Park toward the Brisbane CBD
Pedestrians on the Bicentennial Bikeway view the bridge at dusk

Spectators on the bridge enjoying the 2009
Brisbane Festival and Riverfire celebrations

Night view from Kurilpa Park
Night view over the Riverside Expressway

There can be little doubt that in many ways the story of bridge building is the story of civilisation. By it we can readily measure an important part of a people's progress.
(Franklin D Roosevelt, 1931)

HAIG BECK AND JACKIE COOPER

AN ABRIDGED HISTORY OF BRIDGES

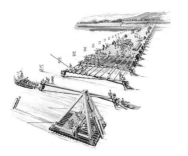

5 Pont du Gard, south of France (c19BC)
6 Puente de Alconétar, Cáceres Province, Spain (c120AD)

1 Roman timber bridge construction

2 The Cloaca Maxima: a vaulted drain running through the Forum in Rome (c600BC)

3 Alcantara Bridge, Cáceres Province, Spain (103–06AD)

4 Demonstration of the load-bearing potential of an arch assembled from wedge-shaped 'voussoirs'

There are bridges, and there are bridges. When we were kids, our special bridges were the timber ones across sand-bottomed coastal estuaries: narrow, single-lane affairs, no handrails, with a deck of weathered hardwood planks the size of railway sleepers that rattled and rumbled when the occasional car drove across. These were bridges that were simultaneously scary and safe, fragile and strong. They spanned transparent green depths, where sunlight bounced back from the sandy river bottom through the silvery flicker of schools of fish, while all around was absolute silence except for the distant roar of the surf. We colonised these timber bridges, armed with our fishing lines, bait tins and sand crab nets. They were the locus of our daily river adventures (the beach was another story) and central to our memories of sunburnt, sandfly-bitten, salt-encrusted summer holidays.

Rivers divide places. It is thus no surprise that bridges, the places of connection, have always held a special place in our collective imaginations. In ancient Greek mythology, it was a river, the Styx, which formed the boundary between the earth and the underworld. For the ancient Romans it was a river, the Tiber, that divided and protected them from the Etruscans; and in doing so, the river assumed sacred connotations. Religious rites associated with bridging the Tiber were conducted by the high-priest, the *pontifex*, 'bridge-builder' (*pontifex* from *pons*: bridge + *facere*: to make). Today the term 'pontiff' (from *pontifex*: high-priest) means bishop. The Pope is the Roman Pontiff, the Bishop of Rome, and the title carries with it distant echoes of one who builds bridges: between heaven and earth.

The Romans took bridge building seriously. The Roman Empire depended on the ability to move armies rapidly across great distances, and the army built roads and bridges to provide a fast and permanent system of communications. When in a hurry, they improvised bridges by lashing barges together, side-by-side, building a bridge deck of logs over them that was paved with compacted clay and straw. With more time at hand, they drove clusters of sharpened logs (piles) into a riverbed and spanned logs between them to form a bridge deck (1). These bridges were feats of military organisation and engineering, and the Romans' 'masonry' bridges were even more so.

Roman masonry bridges were based on the structural principles of the semicircular arch. Semicircular vaults had been used in ancient Egypt and Mesopotamia – usually for drains and ordinary houses, with spans of no more than 2–4 metres (2) – for several thousands of years. The Romans developed the technology of masonry construction to achieve spans of up to 25 metres and adapted the structural principles of the semicircular vault to bridge building (3).

Usually Roman masonry bridges were constructed from 'wedge-shaped' stones (*voussoirs*) of the same size and shape (4). Using this construction technique, the Romans built both 'single-span' bridges and lengthy, 'multiple-arch' bridges (and aqueducts up to three tiers of arches high, such as the Pont du Gard (5) in the south of France). In time they developed segmental arches (such as, just the upper portion of a semicircle). The low, curved bridges made using these arches were both elegant and more efficient: they achieved the required span using less material and with a gentler curve (6). (The practical Romans observed that while semi-circular arches were appropriate to spanning deep ravines, the lower segmental arch was more suited for crossing streams in flatter country.)

While a Roman army had wheeled baggage and supply trains and its cavalry, the foot soldiers (legionnaires) walked, like the rest of the populace. The notion that bridges might be built primarily for vehicles rather than pedestrians is comparatively recent. Until the Industrial Revolution and the advent of the railways, only the very wealthy could afford wheeled transport. Most people walked, and bridges were built principally with them in mind (7).

Medieval habitable bridges seem to have been purpose-designed to capitalise on the concentration of wayfarers at river crossings. Bridges were perfectly positioned to enable shops and businesses to appeal to this captive passing trade. People crossing were necessarily funnelled between the two banks and, importantly, were on foot. When London Bridge was completed in 1209, King John quickly perceived a revenue stream and licensed the building upon the bridge of shops and houses of up to seven storeys (8). In 1345, the Ponte Vecchio in Florence was similarly built with shops and houses on it (9). The Pont de Notre Dame in Paris, begun in 1412, carried 60 houses with shops. The Rialto Bridge in Venice (1591), which replaced earlier timber versions that were in the habit of collapsing, was also lined with shops (10).

. . . in 1209, King John quickly perceived a revenue stream and licensed the building upon the bridge of shops and houses of up to seven storeys

In engineering terms, the Rialto Bridge was the most graceful of them all, with a single span of 29 metres. As a single-span, stone, segmental arch bridge, it rivalled the Mostar Bridge (11), a semicircular arch bridge that also spanned 29 metres (completed a little earlier, in 1566 by the Turkish architect, Mimar Hayruddin; destroyed by the Croatians in 1993, and reconstructed in 2004). Both these were relatively modern versions of the Pont-Saint-Martin, a stone, semicircular-arch bridge with a 31 metre span built by the Romans in northern Italy in the first century BC (12). Apart from some purely aesthetic developments, little had changed in nearly 2000 years of bridge building.

INDUSTRIAL REVOLUTION

Everything changed in 1773 when the English architect Thomas Pritchard proposed a 'single-span', 'cast-iron-arch' bridge across the Severn Gorge near Coalbrookdale in England. Built by Abraham Darby III, an ironmaster working in the Gorge, the bridge was begun in 1778 and completed in 1781. It had a span of 30 metres. The Iron Bridge – the first iron bridge built – marks one of the beginnings of the Industrial Revolution. It is significant in another way: Pritchard's design stripped away much of the redundant material in the bridge's great supporting arch to reveal what Pritchard believed was the pattern of forces acting on the arch as it transferred the load to the abutments on either side (13).

A cast-iron structure on this scale had never before been attempted. The little that was understood about the structural behaviour of this new material had been derived empirically through a series of successful (and sometimes failed) small-scale applications. The size of the members and how they would behave when loaded was largely a matter of educated guesswork; and how the prefabricated parts were to be assembled was also new territory (Pritchard and Darby solved this problem by using jointing techniques borrowed from carpentry).

7 The bridge as a pedestrian domain: the Galata Pontoon Bridge, Istanbul, Turkey (1872)

8 London Bridge (1209) as depicted in a 17th-century engraving

9 Ponte Vecchio, Florence, Italy (1345)

10 Rialto Bridge, Venice, Italy (1591)

11 Mostar Bridge, Mostar, Bosnia and Herzegovina (1566, reconstructed 2004)

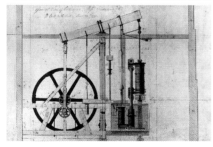

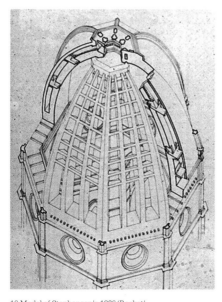

The cast-iron components, by nature brittle owing to their high carbon content, proved strong in compression but weak in tension: once loaded, several bridge members cracked and some even sheared (a few of Darby's wrought-iron band-aid repairs are still in service). Fortunately, the bridge proved to be substantially over-designed: while Darby had used 378 tons of iron to span 30 metres, the slightly later Wearmouth Bridge in Sunderland (opened 1796) required only three-quarters of this weight of iron for the much greater span of 75 metres (14).

The Industrial Revolution that made these iron bridges possible, also saw James Watt's improved designs for the steam engine (1763–75) (15), the first steam-powered locomotive built by Richard Trevithick (1804) and Robert Stephenson's famous Rocket (1829) (16), which in turn led to the development of the railways: the first mass-transport system. Like the earlier Roman roads, networks of railway lines spread across the land. Gradients were necessarily slight, requiring cuttings and tunnels, embankments and bridges capable of carrying the considerable weight of a fully-laden steam train. These bridges were not built with pedestrians in mind. Indeed, in the 19th-century, many of the most innovative of the new bridges were built specifically to carry trains; and the men who designed them were members of a new professional class in Britain: civil engineers.

The great architects of the Renaissance were also its great engineers: we are reminded of Filippo Brunelleschi's design for the dome of the Duomo in Florence (1446–61), with its system of embedded iron chains (17); Leonardo da Vinci's many inventions and engineering designs including a proposal for an arched bridge with a single span of 240 metres across the Golden Horn in Turkey (1502); Andrea Palladio's description of timber truss bridges in his treatise on architecture, *I Quattro Libri dell'Architettura* (published 1570); and Christopher Wren, astronomer, mathematician, physicist, engineer and the architect of St Paul's Cathedral, London, with its structurally ingenious treble dome (1673–1710). Thomas Pritchard, the designer of the 'Iron' Bridge, was an architect too; and even Thomas Telford, the first president of the Institute of Engineers in Britain and the designer of the second iron bridge across the Severn (1796), was an architect (who initially trained as a stone mason).

Increasing demand for large-span bridges to speed communications and facilitate commerce caused bridge design to become part of a new discipline: civil engineering (distinct from military engineering or architecture). The essentially utilitarian purpose of many of these bridges, and the fact that they were speculative developments, made cost an important consideration. The amount of iron (by weight) in the Iron Bridge, for example, represented about two-thirds of its final cost. For engineers, the weight of a structure became a measure of its cost-effectiveness, and in time, a measure of its engineering elegance.

ENGINEER'S AESTHETIC

The English landscape and social economy of the late 18th-century underwent transformations effected by unprecedented, new industrial forms: steam engines, mechanised looms, iron bridges: an industrial revolution driven by machines and structures conceived and built by engineers. The British engineering tradition had two central attributes: empiricism, and the drive for economy. Empiricism – or working from practice towards theory – leads to testing and experimentation, out

12 Pont-Saint-Martin, Aosta Valley, Italy (1st century BC)
13 Thomas Pritchard and Abraham Darby III: Iron Bridge, Coakbrookdale, England (1778–81)
14 First Wearmouth Bridge, Sunderland, England (1796)
15 Boulton and Watt's design for a steam engine (1769)

16 Model of Stephenson's 1829 'Rocket'
17 Cut-away drawing of Filippo Brunelleschi's design for the dome of the Duomo, Florence, Italy (1446–61)

of which design solutions evolve. British engineers worked by 'trial and error' to construct the first steam engines, shipping canals and iron bridges.

Just as the master builders of Gothic cathedrals learnt empirically from the lessons of collapsing spires how best to resist the invisible forces of gravity, so 19th-century engineers advanced their technical knowledge through practical experimentation. While the cathedral builders were inspired to dematerialise the heavy masonry walls of cathedrals and raise stone spires heavenwards, 19th-century engineers and the industrialists who commissioned them, were motivated by a grounded desire for economic efficiency: to achieve the most favourable power-to-weight ratio in order to produce maximum force using minimal fuel; to resist stresses with the least amount of material; to ensure that nothing was superfluous or redundant. The Modernist design mantra 'Less is more' could equally have been the motto of both the Gothic master builders and the engineers of the 19th-century.

18 An early 18th-century beam engine used for draining a Cornish mine

19 Isambard Kingdom Brunel: Clifton Suspension Bridge, near Bristol, England (designed: 1830; built: 1862–64)

The engineering tradition was steered by rationalism, technical experimentation and the economical use of materials

The engineering tradition was steered by rationalism, technical experimentation and the economical use of materials; and these concerns tended to produce results of a pronounced elegance. The elegance is epitomised in the design of the giant steam-powered beam engines (18) that drained the coalmines that fuelled England's 'satanic mills'. The makers of these machines exposed every working member, nuts and bolts and all. Nothing was covered up. All aspects of the workings – the parts and their motions – were exposed not merely as a matter of economic expediency: they were consciously displayed. To see such machinery in motion was simultaneously to understand how it worked. The graceful dance of the massive engines – with the steady rise and fall of shiny piston rods, the gentle rocking motion of the massive iron beam and the counter, eye-blurring whirl of the finely articulated governor – was intrinsic to a new aesthetic of the machine. Each part was pared down to the threshold of structural integrity and precision-tooled. Every element – from the smallest screw to the largest member – had a reductive elegance that revealed the nature of the material it was crafted from, the craftsmanship required to fashion it, and the manner in which it was connected to and acted on the other parts. We now recognise the design sensibility expressed here as the engineer's aesthetic.

Whether they were arch, truss or suspension, iron bridges in the 19th-century – in their stripped-back tracery of metal – expressed the designer's understanding of the forces in play. With experience, redundancy was progressively trimmed to reveal a skeleton of structure clearly resisting the pressures acting on it. In bridge building, it became the grail to reveal the structure in all its elemental essentials and in their lightest (and therefore most economical) possible arrangement, resisting the loads acting on it to achieve stasis: a delicate and stable balance between all the forces (what Le Corbusier termed 'harmony').

The designers of iron bridges built between 1840 and 1870 overcame the brittleness problem, by using cast iron for compression members and malleable wrought iron (with a very low carbon content) for tension members. While the cast-iron

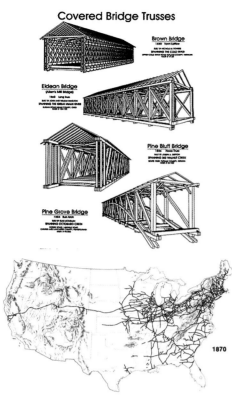

Covered Bridge Trusses

Brown Bridge
1880 Town Lattice
BUILT BY NICHOLAS M. POWERS
SPANNING THE COLD RIVER
UPPER COLD RIVER ROAD SHREWSBURY, RUTLAND COUNTY, VERMONT

Eldean Bridge
(Allen's Mill Bridge)
1845 Long Truss
BUILT BY JOHN AND WILLIAM DALGORN
SPANNING THE GREAT MIAMI RIVER
ELDEAN ROAD TROY, MIAMI COUNTY, OHIO

Pine Bluff Bridge
1884 Howe Truss
BUILT BY JOSEPH A. BRITTON
SPANNING BIG WALNUT CREEK
HOME ROAD HARLEM SPRINGS TOWNSHIP, CARROLL COUNTY, OHIO

Pine Grove Bridge
1884 Burr Arch
BUILT BY ELIAS McMELLEN
SPANNING OCTORARO CREEK
PROVIDENCE TOWNSHIP, LANCASTER COUNTY, PENNSYLVANIA

1870

20 Timber trusses used in the construction of American covered bridges

21 Railroad network in the USA (1870)

22 Wilburton Trestle Bridge, Washington, USA (built: 1904; rebuilt several times since)

23 Restored wrought-iron Pratt truss bridge

> Many of these bridges were based on 'king and queen' post trusses used by carpenters since medieval times to roof barns and churches.

compression members remained reassuringly sturdy, the more costly wrought-iron tension members became increasingly finer and lighter. Thus, functional and economic considerations, made manifest the pushing and pulling forces in play.

CULTURAL CONTRASTS

In Britain, the requirement for bridge structures to be functional and economical was compounded by demands for style. The bridges Brunel and Telford built were expressive demonstrations of the revolutionary technologies and new industrial techniques of the era. In addition, they also stylistically reflected a contradictory 'nostalgic' trend in British society, that longed for a return to an imagined simpler pre-industrial age. The stone abutments and pylons designed for bridges were styled as medieval castles and Gothic spires; and the ornate detailing of the ironwork relied on the pre-industrial artisan skills of the iron foundry craftsmen.

In the United States, where good structural timber was still readily available in the early 19th-century, most bridges were constructed with timber. Many of these bridges were based on 'king and queen' post trusses used by carpenters since medieval times to roof barns and churches. These bridges were often enclosed (as in *The Bridges of Madison County*) to protect the timber trusses and considerably extend their life (20).

The first railroads were built in the United States at about the same time as railroads were laid down in Britain, but it was not until the 1850s that the length of track began to grow rapidly and follow the nation's westward continental expansion: from 65 kilometres in 1830 to more than 65,000 kilometres in 1865, at the end of the Civil War (21). As new territory was opened up for settlement, the returns to railroad speculators became so substantial, that American railroad engineers raced to lay track, temporarily spanning obstacles in the way with timber trestle structures. Many of these trestle bridges were substantial: the Wilburton Trestle in Washington was a towering framework more than 30 metres high (22). These structures were not built to last, and in time most were replaced by embankments or more permanent bridges.

Unlike Britain – where engineers could rely on the skills of artisans steeped in craft traditions – in the American Wild West there were few stonemasons and ironworkers. American engineers developed designs using simply jointed modular components, that could be assembled by unskilled labour. When it came to larger span bridges, these engineers turned to the familiar timber truss structures dotted throughout the North American landscape. Initially they developed longer and more efficient trusses by combining timber compression members with wrought-iron tension rods. As loads and spans increased, they experimented with more complex trusses that combined cast and wrought iron.

From the 1850s, all-metal trusses began to dominate the design of permanent railroad bridges (not only in America, but in Britain too). Several truss designs were patented, each enjoying a degree of popularity before a newer and more efficient model was introduced. Two early timber trusses were adapted to iron construction: the Howe truss (patented in 1840) had vertical tension members and diagonal compression members; in the similar Pratt truss (invented in 1844), the vertical members were in compression (23). The Warren truss (patented in 1848) had no vertical members, but a zigzag configuration of diagonal members arranged as equilateral triangles, alternately in compression and tension, as they approach the centre of the span (24). The Bollman truss (patented in 1852) used a multiplicity of tension members to avoid catastrophic failure (25). And the Fink truss (designed in Germany by Albert Fink in the 1860s) separated out compression and tension members in a particularly elegant and reductive arrangement (26).

Many American railroad bridges were mass-produced, often manufactured half a continent away from where they were to be erected. With an eye to economy, they were prefabricated from repetitive elements free of ornament and with uncomplicated connections that made them easy to assemble. Compared to British bridges of the time, these American bridges revealed an engineering aesthetic that was functional, practical and redolent of the utilitarian can-do pragmatism that typified pioneering 19th-century American society.

It would be unfair to suggest that Americans did not design beautiful bridges or that British-designed bridges were not functional; but differing culturally formed perceptions about the relative efficacy of craftsmanship versus mass-production were in play. Even in 20th-century civil engineering works we can still recognise an aesthetic dichotomy between the European and North American engineering traditions; between the rhetorical and the utilitarian. Nor would it be fair to suggest that the Americans 'owned' the truss bridge. The lenticular truss – in which the top and bottom chords of the truss arched, forming a lens shape – was patented in America in 1878 by William Douglas; but by 1850, Brunel had developed this truss form for his Royal Albert Bridge, in which the heavy tubular top chord is in compression and the wrought-iron chains that form the bottom chord are in tension (27).

STRUCTURAL INNOVATIONS

On both sides of the Atlantic, the Industrial Revolution fuelled the commercial intercourse that transformed local economies into national economies and towns into cities. These towns, located on rivers in the days of water transport, found themselves divided as they grew; and the natural barriers between regions tended to restrict the growth of national commerce. Wheeled transport (not only trains) was becoming increasingly 'the norm'. Bridges were in demand, and in many places, very big bridges with very large spans over very extreme terrain.

Innovation marked the approach of the newly-minted civil engineers to the problems of building large spans at great heights and on difficult foundations. Suspension bridges were an important breakthrough. Rope suspension bridges were well known (the Incas had built grass-rope suspension footbridges; they had no wheeled vehicles) (28). The problem with these bridges was that in time the ropes sagged and so did the deck. In 1800 in Pennsylvania, an American judge, James Finley, solved this problem with his wrought-iron chain suspension bridge that incorporated a truss to give the horizontal deck rigidity (29). The chain 'links' were wrought-iron bars (strong in tension) with links forged at each end. Finley built 13 of these bridges, patenting his design in 1808.

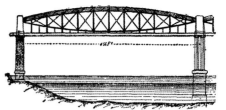

24 Modern Warrant truss bridge, USA

25 Wrought-and cast-iron Bollman truss bridge, Savage, Maryland, USA (1869)

26 Wrought-and cast-iron Fink truss bridge, Hamden, New Jersey, USA (1857)

27 Lenticular truss developed by Brunel for the Royal Albert Bridge, Saltash, England (1854–59)

28 The last surviving Inca suspension bridge, Peru (the bridge is rebuilt every few years by the local villagers)

29 Engraving of one of James Finley's wrought-iron chain suspension bridges, USA (published in 1810)

30 Joseph Chaley: Grand Pont Suspendu, Fribourg, Switzerland (1830–34)

31 Thomas Telford: Manai Strait road bridge, Wales (1926)

32 Robert Stephenson: Britannia Railway Bridge, Menai Strait, Wales (1845–50)

33 Britannia Railway Bridge wrought-iron box section structure

34 Isambard Kingdom Brunel: Royal Albert Bridge, Saltash, England (1854–59)

35 Charles Ellet: Wheeling suspension bridge over the Ohio River, USA (1847–49; shown after being rebuilt)

The first 'wire-cable' suspension bridge was also built in Pennsylvania (1816). The first 'modern' aerial-spun wrought-iron wire-cable bridge was the Grand Pont Suspendu at Fribourg, Switzerland, with a span of 273 metres (1830–34), designed by a French army medical officer turned engineer, Joseph Chaley (30). In Britain, around 1815, Thomas Telford experimented with wrought-iron bar and wire-cable suspension systems, subjecting them to extensive tensile testing. (These tests mark one of the beginnings of a more 'scientific' approach to bridge design in Britain.) Then in 1818 Telford applied these ideas to his design for the Menai Strait road bridge in Wales, completed in 1826, with a suspended chain-span of 176 metres (31).

Robert Stephenson's 'Britannia Railway' Bridge across the Menai Strait (1845–50) was a continuous, riveted iron-plate rectangular tube – a giant box beam in two spans of 144 metre each – with the train lines within (32). In settling on a box beam structure (33), Stephenson consulted Eaton Hodgkinson, a prominent theorist, on the strength of materials (the scientific approach to structural design was by now gaining ground over the purely empirical).

As bridge spans increased, so did the problem of building suitable foundations. To build bridge foundations in mid-stream, the Romans developed cofferdams from a double perimeter of log piles made watertight with clay filling in the gap between them. Water was bailed out, and with the riverbed now exposed, foundations were dug. To cross the Tamar River (the eastern border of Cornwall), Brunel had to locate the central pier of his Royal Albert Bridge, Saltash (1853–59), on a riverbed nearly 25 metre below high water – beyond the reach of any cofferdam. Brunel's solution was to use a cast-iron caisson – a bottomless, watertight chamber filled with compressed air – from which the construction work on the pier could be carried out underwater. The bridge structure was also innovative, with a design that combined the structural characteristics of suspension, arch and truss into a single unified form in two spans of nearly 140 metre each (34).

As bridge spans increased, so did the problem of building suitable foundations.

While the Industrial Revolution did not begin in France until after the Napoleonic Wars (c1815), the professional discipline of engineering was already established: the École nationale des ponts et chaussées (National School of Bridges and Roads) was founded in 1747 specifically to train engineers. When the Industrial Revolution did arrive, France's engineers were already versed in theoretical analysis of structure and materials. (In the early 1820s, the young Brunel had gone to Paris to study engineering, but as a foreigner, had been denied entry: France at that time led suspension bridge engineering.)

Charles Ellet, as a young American, did gain access to the École nationale des ponts et chaussées in the early 1830s. He returned to the USA, French-trained and schooled in the latest 'wire-cable' suspension technology, to build the Fairmont Bridge (1838–41). This – America's first long-span 109 metre wire-cable suspension bridge – was followed by Ellet's Wheeling Suspension Bridge (1847–49), spanning 308 metres over the Ohio River (35). Ellet theorised that the flexibility of wire-cable suspension bridges, together with the greater deck weight of large spans and the shallow profile that the deck presented to wind forces, would make them inherently stable in high winds. He was wrong: in a violent storm in 1854, the bridge twisted and undulated until it collapsed. Ellet's technologically sophisticated wire-cable suspension structure made great spans possible, but it revealed another problem: the effects of wind loading.

A wire-cable suspension railroad bridge across Niagara Falls (1851–55), designed and built by John Roebling, overcame the structural problems revealed in the Wheeling Bridge with a bridge deck formed as a deep truss (36). A railroad ran on top of the truss, while enclosed within the truss (constructed with timber compression members) was a lower deck for a roadway. What engineers at the time failed to fully appreciate was that in suspension bridges, the stiffening result of a deeper road deck structure was a crucial factor in resisting the vibrating effects of wind loading. Roebling's second contribution to the design of wire-cable suspension bridges was to compact the wire strands (there were 3640 in each of the four cables) into continuous, tightly-packed cylinders wrapped with more wire.

STEEL BRIDGES

Apart from highlighting the pragmatic nature of the American engineering aesthetic, Roebling's choice of timber for the compression members was in fact no choice: the weight of cast iron required to achieve the same structural effect would have been prohibitive in a suspension bridge. The bridge designs of Roebling and his peers were constrained by the inherent brittleness (and consequent weakness) of cast iron. Wrought iron ('worked' iron) was processed to reduce impurities (particularly the metal's carbon content), to overcome this deficiency. However, contrary to the demands of economical mass-production in an industrial age, the process, known as forging, was complex, lengthy and required highly skilled labour.

To make steel economically and in quantity, was one of the technological challenges of the Industrial Revolution.

Compared to cast and wrought iron, steel (an alloy of iron with a low carbon content and traces of other alloy elements) combines superior qualities of hardness, tensile strength and ductility (this latter characteristic making it relatively easy to draw into wire, roll into very thin plates, or cast without affecting its inherent qualities of hardness and tensile strength). Steel had long been recognised for these qualities, particularly for making swords: Hannibal's army used Toledo-forged steel swords against the Romans. Unfortunately, steel was even more difficult and expensive to make than wrought iron. To remove the impurities from the iron and introduce the appropriate alloy elements required numerous forgings (the ancient Chinese called it the 'hundred refinings method').

To make steel economically and in quantity, was one of the technological challenges of the Industrial Revolution. In 1855 the British inventor Henry Bessemer patented the Bessemer process that used the oxygen in air blown through molten pig iron to burn off the impurities, to create steel from iron ore, in just a two-step process (37). Bessemer was responding to an armaments problem: the British Army's cast-iron big guns couldn't withstand the forces generated by a new type of artillery shell Bessemer had invented. And it wasn't only cast-iron big guns that were failing catastrophically. So were some of the most significant cast-iron bridges of the day. In Britain they included the Dee Bridge (built in 1846, collapsed in 1847, killing five people); the Bull Bridge (built in 1837, collapsed in 1860); the Wootton Bridge

36 John Roebling: Niagara Falls Bridge, USA (1851–55)
37 Henry Bessemer's original Bessemer forge (1855)
38 News of the Tay Bridge disaster (1879)

39 James Eads: St Louis Bridge across the Mississippi River, USA (1867–74)

40 Benjamin Baker and John Fowler: Forth Bridge, Scotland (1882–90)

41 John Roebling (with Washington Roebling and Emily Warren Roebling): Brooklyn Bridge, New York, USA (1867–83)

James Eads' St Louis Bridge across the Mississippi River (1867–74) is probably the first truly 'modern' bridge

(built in 1844, collapsed in 1861, killing two people); and the Tay Bridge (built in 1878, collapsed in 1879, killing 60 people). And in the USA there was the Ashtabula Bridge disaster (built in 1865, collapsed in 1876, killing 90 people). In all these cases, failure was due to the brittleness of the cast-iron members (aggravated in the case of the Tay Bridge disaster (38) by the designer's failure to make allowances for wind loadings).

James Eads' St Louis Bridge across the Mississippi River (1867–74) is probably the first truly 'modern' bridge: the first major steel structure and the first to use a cantilevered arch (doing away with the need to erect a temporary structure to support the tubular steel arches during construction; an important development considering the fast-flowing Mississippi). To build the bridge piers, Eade had to penetrate 25 metres of Mississippi mud to reach bedrock. His solution was to use caissons and compressed air (as had Brunel for his Royal Albert Bridge), though with a difference: while workers carried out the excavation at the bottom of the caisson, the masonry pier was simultaneously built above them, its great weight forcing the caisson ever deeper into the mud. (Working in a compressed air environment was hazardous: 15 men died from 'caisson disease', the decompression disease we now recognise as 'the bends'.) Completed, the St Louis Bridge had three arches – each with a span of more than 150 metres – with a two-lane road on top and a single railroad below (39).

The second significant steel bridge of the era was the Forth Bridge (1882–90), the long-rail bridge spanned the Firth of Forth (40). Designed by Benjamin Baker and John Fowler, it was also a cantilever structure. Importantly, the Forth Bridge marks the moment when 'scientific' engineering came of age: not only did Baker design the bridge based on his calculations of the stresses in the completed structure, but he also pioneered the calculation of erection stresses: (in a cantilevered structure these are very different from the stresses in the completed spans), wind pressure stresses and temperature stresses. Each of the two main spans, at 521 metre, consists of two cantilevered trusses with a suspended truss between them. The Forth Bridge also had a new aesthetic dimension: following the Tay Bridge disaster, Baker and Fowler set about building a 'stiff' bridge, one that structurally and visibly resists gale-force winds. (Erecting this massive steel structure at up to 100 metres above the water was hazardous: nearly 100 workers were killed and many hundreds seriously injured.)

The first steel wire-cable suspension bridge was the Brooklyn Bridge (1867–83). At the time its span, at 486 metres, was 50 per cent longer than any previous bridge (41). The bridge was designed by John Roebling – of the Niagara Falls Bridge fame – and built by his son, Washington, who was partially paralysed from the bends, following a site inspection of one of the caissons. For the following 11 years, his wife Emily Warren Roebling assisted him by supervising its construction. To this end, she undertook the study of higher mathematics, catenary curve calculations, the strength of materials, bridge specifications and wire-cable construction – a measure of how far 'scientific' bridge design had come. (While the effect of wind on large-span suspension bridges was not fully understood, the open truss structure of the bridge deck, reduced the aerodynamic problems caused by wind loadings.)

TWENTIETH CENTURY

In the early 20th-century, the invention of the automobile and the mass mobility it facilitated, resulted in rapid expansion of the highway network in America. As in the 19th-century when the country was building its railroads, America suddenly found itself divided again by wide rivers, broad expanses of water and deep ravines, all of which had to be bridged.

Because trains generated considerable point loads, designers usually favoured sturdy arch and truss structures for railway bridges: suspension bridges being considered too flimsy and 'lively'. However, the lighter loads of road traffic made the suspension bridge a more economical alternative, particularly for very large spans. In the 19th-century, the design of iron arch and truss bridges had been bedevilled by the unpredictable brittleness of cast iron; in the 20th-century, a problem for designers would be, the seemingly unpredictable effects of wind loads on suspension bridges.

At the same time, cantilevered steel arch and cantilevered steel truss bridges were built with increasing spans and reduced amounts of steel. From Roman times, arch bridges had been built with the bridge deck above the supporting arch. Gustav Lindenthal's design for the Hell Gate Bridge in New York (1912–16) suspended the bridge deck below the arch (42). The Sydney Harbour Bridge (1924–32) is based on the same structural principle (43). While the Hell Gate Bridge, with a span of 310 metres, required nearly 40,000 tons of steel, the Sydney Harbour Bridge required slightly less steel to span 503 metres. Initially, the quest to reduce the weight of steel in bridges arose out of the need to reduce costs, but in time it also became an aesthetic. As the 20th-century proceeded, bridge structures became increasingly finer, with trusses more airy and bridge decks ever thinner.

This new lightweight aesthetic was particularly evident in the design of suspension bridges. The first step was to build bridges with towers of steel instead of masonry. Several were built in this new fashion. The turning point was the George Washington Bridge in New York (1927–31): at that time, it was the longest span in the world 1100 metres; the original deck depth-to-span ratio was an astonishingly slender 1:350 (in 1962 a lower-level deck was added, considerably reducing this ratio); and the tracery of criss-cross steel bracing forming the towers was left exposed (44). The designers had originally intended the steel as the reinforcing for the massive concrete towers clad in granite. Their change of heart was partly in response to the Depression-inspired cost-cutting, but also in response to growing public appreciation of the stripped, abstracted aesthetics of Functionalist Modernism.

The need to stiffen the decks of suspension bridges to resist the vibrating and oscillating effects of wind, was by now, better understood. For bridges with very long spans and wide decks, the support that deep beams (plate girders) provided under the deck was sufficient to resist these forces. Bridges with much narrower decks needed additional stiffening, usually with a deep truss under the deck, as the Golden Gate Bridge required (1933–37, span: 1280 metres) (45).

Leon Moisseiff, one of the designers of the Golden Gate Bridge, theorised that a thin, flexible bridge deck would flex in the wind, reducing stresses by transmitting forces via the suspension cables to the bridge towers. Moisseiff applied his 'deflection theory' to the design of the Tacoma Narrows Bridge in Washington State (1937–40). The bridge had a span of over 850 metres and a 'plate-girder' deck with a

42 Gustav Lindenthal: Hell Gate Bridge, New York, USA (1912–16)

43 Ralph Freeman: Sydney Harbour Bridge, Australia (1924–32)

44 George Washington Bridge, New York, USA (1927–31)

45 Charles Alton Ellis and Leon Moisseiff (with architect, Irving Morrow): Golden Gate Bridge, San Francisco, USA (1933–37)

46 Leon Moisseiff's Tacoma Narrows Bridge, Washington

47 News of the Tacoma Narrows Bridge collapse (1940) in State, USA (1937–40).

depth-to-span ratio of 1:350 (46). The deck, however, was very narrow: only two lanes wide. Four months after it was opened, the bridge dramatically blew down in strong winds, after it began to vibrate and then undulate in a self-exciting oscillation, known as aeroelastic flutter (47). (The event was captured on 16mm film and has been essential viewing for engineering and architecture students ever since.)

BEAUTIFUL BRIDGES

The manner of the destruction of the Tacoma Narrows Bridge was not wholly unexpected. Since Roman times, soldiers have been taught to break step when marching over bridges. In 1850 the Basse-Chaîne suspension bridge in France (1836–39) collapsed, resulting in the deaths of 226 troops marching in step over it. In 1854 the Wheeling Suspension Bridge spanning the Ohio River started undulating severely in a storm and collapsed. Roebling, who was building the Niagara suspension bridge at the time, immediately took precautions to tie his bridge deck down with guy-wires anchored to the adjacent cliff-face. Not only was Moisseiff aware of this history, he also understood the physical phenomenon, and his 'deflection theory' was a response to it. So why did his Tacoma Narrows Bridge blow apart?

Before its collapse, Moisseiff called his Tacoma Narrows design 'the most beautiful bridge in the world'. His statement reveals the degree to which engineering design had become aestheticised. Like his fellow engineers, Moisseiff's approach to design was based on a simple utilitarian principle: minimising the weight of steel in a project reduced its cost. But Moisseiff took this to extremes.

The Tacoma Narrows Bridge was designed at the moment when the European doctrine of Functionalist Modernism swept America. Inventive, progressive and optimistic in spirit, it matched the American 'can-do' character. At a popular level, 'Art Deco' and 'jazz' epitomised the new Modern age, colouring American music, movies and mass-produced objects of everyday life. On another level, American artists and designers applied the aesthetics of Modernism – abstraction and reductivism – to their work. This Modernist American zeitgeist encompassed popular culture, art and industry, science and technology.

America was also in the middle of the Great Depression, and under President Roosevelt's New Deal programme (1933–36), vast infrastructure projects featuring dams and bridges were being built. The engineering grandeur of these projects – the slender elegance of the Golden Gate suspension bridge (1933–37), the massive beauty of the Hoover Dam (1931–36) – captured the national imagination (48).

'Scientific' engineering had made considerable advances since the 19th-century, but to build bridges and dams on the scale demanded by the New Deal, still required much daring guesswork by engineers: hunches and hypotheses dressed-up as theories (like Moisseiff's intuitive, but fatal 'deflection theory'). Engineers may have been the new heroes, but they too were infected by Modernism's aesthetics. In this context, it is hard to view Moisseiff as a negligent villain; he was more the victim of profession-wide hubris and also of the times.

Chastened by the design misadventure of the Tacoma Narrows Bridge, American engineers returned to stiffening the decks of suspension bridges with deep (yet elegant, airy) trusses (49). British engineers, however, persisted with the quest for

48 Hoover (Boulder) Dam, Colorado River, USA (1931–36)

49 David Steinman: Mackinac Bridge, Michigan, USA (1953–57) showing the trussed deck under construction

50 Freeman, Fox and Partners: Severn Bridge, England (1961–66)

Before its collapse, Moisseiff called his Tacoma Narrows design 'the most beautiful bridge in the world'.

ever more slender decks: instead of relying on the stiffening effect of deep supporting steel beams (plate girders), they made the decks much shallower, but considerably stiffer, welded-steel hollow box beams (50). In America, engineers relied on the open filigree of the trusses to act as wind spoilers, creating eddies and wind disturbances to dampen the harmonic vibrations that had destroyed the Tacoma Narrows Bridge. On the other side of the Atlantic, engineers took the opposite tack of minimising wind resistance, using wind tunnel testing to develop bridge decks with thin, 'aerofoil-like' profiles (51).

During the 1930s, some of the most beautiful bridges in the world were being built in Europe, not in America, in reinforced concrete to designs by the Swiss engineer Robert Maillart. Concrete, used by the Romans (52), was a lost technology after the fall of the Roman Empire until the mid-18th-century. Concrete was 'rediscovered' (reinvented) by John Smeaton and used in his design for the Eddystone Lighthouse (1756–59) (53). Technical advances in the 19th-century, particularly the use of wrought iron and then steel reinforcing, led to its use in bridges.

CONCRETE BRIDGES

Two of Maillart's early bridges were important aesthetic and conceptual design breakthroughs. The Zouz Bridge (1901) – a small 30 metre 'single-span' reinforced concrete segmental arch in Switzerland – was significant for two reasons: it was the first hollow-concrete 'box-beam' bridge and (even more significant) the first concrete bridge to express concrete-as-concrete rather than faux masonry (54). This was an aesthetic design decision that slightly predates the first truthful expression of concrete in architecture (Frank Lloyd Wright's Unity Temple in Chicago and Auguste Perret's Garage Ponthieu in Paris, both designed 1905), and marks this bridge as one of the first structures of the early Modern Movement.

In 1905 Maillart designed the Tavanasa Bridge, another reinforced concrete segmental arch, spanning the Rhine (55). In the earlier Zouz Bridge, he had noted some cracking in the (structurally redundant) concrete adjacent to the spring points of the ach. In the Tavanasa Bridge he avoided this superficial, but unsightly problem by removing structurally redundant material from the design. Conceptually, this was similar to the 'first' iron bridge (1773–81), where redundant material in the bridge's great supporting arch was stripped out to reveal what the designer, Pritchard, believed was the pattern of forces acting upon it.

Maillart's genius lay in his ability to visualise the forces acting on a structure and exploit the plastic nature of concrete to realise it. He designed bridges in which the deck, the deck supports, the arch and its stiffening ribs together formed, an efficient, integrated structural whole, composed from the thinnest possible planes of reinforced concrete. Maillart was an engineer's engineer who achieved what his American contemporary, Moisseiff (both were born in 1872), aspired to: bridge designs expressing the structure with absolute aesthetic clarity, while using the bare minimum of material. (Robert Maillart did succeed in designing the 'most beautiful bridge in the world': in 2001 a worldwide survey of the readers of the British journal *Bridge Design and Engineering* voted his Salginatobel Bridge in Switzerland the most beautiful bridge of the 20th-century.)

The design for the Salginatobel Bridge (1929–30) was selected from 19 submissions (not because of its beauty: infact the selection panel didn't like its form; they chose

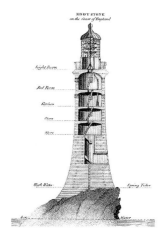

51 Severn Bridge showing the box-beam bridge deck with its aerofoil-like profile

52 Roman concrete: Baths of Caracalla, Rome, Italy (212–16)

53 John Smeaton: concrete Eddystone Lighthouse, England (1756–59)

54 Robert Maillart: reinforced concrete Zouz Bridge, Switzerland (1901)

55 Robert Maillart: reinforced concrete Tavanasa Bridge, Rhine River, Germany (1905)

56 Robert Maillart: reinforced concrete Salginatobel Bridge, Switzerland (1929–30)

57 Salginatobel Bridge open box girder structure

58 Eugène Fressinet: prestressed concrete Annet sur Marne Bridge, France (1949)

59 Kochertalbrücke (Kocher Valley Bridge): prestressed concrete box beam autobahn bridge, Germany (1976–79)

60 Akashi-Kaiky Bridge, Japan (1988–98): The 1995 Kobe earthquake had its epicentre right between the two towers of the bridge. The original planned length was 1990m for the main span, but the seismic event moved the towers apart by almost a metre. Since construction of the deck had not yet begun, the change was easily accommodated in the slightly altered final design.

61 Tatara Bridge, Japan (1990–99)

it because it was the cheapest to build). While the bridge is only 133 metres long with a span of about 90 metres, its narrow single-lane road deck soars spectacularly 90 metres above the floor of the gorge (56). Just six men built it, and all the concrete was mixed on site and placed by hand. The wafer-thin supporting arch expressively spreads its load at each end, gracefully narrowing towards the centre of the span. The apparent thinness of the arch is achieved by locating the two stiffening ribs in from the outer edge, with the arch and the ribs acting in concert to form an open box-beam (57).

The next development in concrete bridge technology was prestressing. Prestressing permits a concrete member to carry a greater load or to span a greater distance than standard reinforced concrete. Concrete is strong in compression, but weak in tension, so steel reinforcing bars (strong in tension) are located in concrete structures where tensile stresses are to be resisted. When these reinforcing bars are stretched (by being tightened from each end of a structural member), the concrete they pass though is compressed: a process known as 'prestressing'. Prestressing produces compressive stress that can offset the tensile stresses that occur when the member is subsequently loaded.

Prestressing concrete was an idea that had been around since the 1870s, but the technology was not developed until the 1930s, by the French engineer Eugène Fressinet. (Fressinet had made his reputation as a bridge designer in 1907, shortly after graduating from the École nationale des ponts et chaussées, when he built three concrete bridges for the price of one, made from masonry.) After World War II he finally got to build five matching prestressed concrete bridges across the Marne (58), and these opened the way for the vast number of prestressed concrete structures – both buildings and bridges – built since. With prestressing, not only do steel and concrete became almost interchangeable as structural materials, but also prestressed concrete bridges of immense size and great elegance – such as, the Kochertalbrücke in Germany (1976–79) – could be realised (59).

BIG BRIDGES

Since the late 1960s, a series of really big bridges has been constructed. These bridges span, not only very large rivers and broad estuaries, but also the straits and seas that divide countries and continents. For really big spans, suspension bridges have been the answer, but for smaller 'big' spans, cable-stayed bridges have proved less risky, more economical and structurally stable.

The largest bridge project completed so far, is the Japanese scheme to link the island of Shikoku, with a system of 18 bridges across the Inland Sea to the main island, Honshu (1976–99). These bridges follow three routes that hop from island to island on their way across the sea. Both suspension and cable-stayed structures are incorporated into each route. One of the bridges, the Akashi-Kaiky Bridge (1988–98, with a span of 1991 metre), has the longest span of a suspension bridge in the world (60); the Tatara Bridge (1990–99, with a span of 890 metre) had, until recently, the longest span for a cable-stayed bridge in the world (61).

A cable-stayed bridge typically consists of one or more pylons, with cables supporting the bridge deck. They tend to be of two types: fan, where all the cables radiate from the top of the pylon; and harp, where the cables are attached at intervals along the height of the pylon. The cables are stretched forward to support the main span. Countervailing backstays may support an approach span or be anchored to the approach structure. Cable-stayed bridges are constructed by cantilevering the bridge deck out from the base of the pylon, with the cables acting as both temporary supports to the deck during construction and permanent supports when the bridge is built. When the bridge is completed, the bridge deck must be reinforced to resist horizontal compressive stresses along the length of the deck – stresses not encountered in the decks of suspension bridges. Consequently, the decks of cable-stayed bridges are necessarily much 'stiffer' than those of suspension bridges (and therefore they more readily resist the vibrating and oscillating effects of wind and foot traffic that have dogged the design of suspension bridges for nearly 200 years).

62 Roland Mason Ordish: Albert Bridge, London, England (1873); designed as a cable-stayed bridge, but structurally modified to include wrought-iron suspension chains in 1884

> Cable-stayed bridges are inherently elegant owing to the sculptural potential of the pylons

German engineers looking for inexpensive designs to rebuild the many river crossings over the Rhine destroyed during World War II, pioneered the design of modern 'cable-stayed' bridges. (The concept of the cable-stayed bridge had been around since the early 17th-century; and the Albert Bridge in London (1871–73) is one of several 19th-century suspension bridges that incorporated wrought-iron cable stays, to provide additional support for the bridge deck (62). However, until the mid-20th-century, neither the analytical tools required in the design of cable-stayed bridges nor the high-strength wire cable technology required for their construction, was available.)

Relative to other structures, cable-stayed bridges are safer (multiple cables result in a high degree of redundancy): they are highly efficient in their use of materials; they are quick to build; cables are easy to maintain and replace; decks and towers can be fabricated from concrete or steel, or a composite of the two; and decks can be made structurally 'stiff', while still achieving depth-to-span ratios as high as 1:250.

Moisseiff's desire to design the 'most beautiful bridge in the world' reminds us that many engineers are also artists. However, their lot as artists is difficult: engineers generally must play servant to an architect's vision and see their artistry concealed behind a cloak of architectural finishes. But in the case of bridges, the engineer leads the design team.

POETIC BEGINNINGS

Cable-stayed bridges were the answer to the bridge designers' dreams. Big-span cable-stayed bridges – with their giant scale, slender proportions and clarity in expression of structural principles – are very dramatic. And although suspension bridges require two sets of cables to support the deck – and this limits the geometry of the towers to a pair of vertical, cross-braced legs – no such constraint limits the design of pylons for cable-stayed bridges. Cable-stayed bridges are inherently elegant owing to the sculptural potential of the pylons; especially when these are contrasted with the simple thin line of the deck. The form of the pylons and the configuration of the cables seem open to endless design variations; also, being suited to large-span applications, these bridges are frequently located in scenic (even sublime) settings.

For much of the 20th-century, bridge design conformed to a Functionalist aesthetic. Functionalism produces a stark and unambiguous aesthetic, devoid of ornament and poetic embellishment. The Functionalist aesthetic complements the engineering sensibility, which values an abstracted minimalism that reveals structural clarity

63 Franz Dischinger: Strömsund Bridge, Sweden (1956)

64 Egon Eiermann and Sep Ruf: German Pavilion footbridge, Expo 58, Brussels, Belgium

65 Beaulieu, Trudeau et Associés: Pont des îles, Expo 67, Montréal, Canada (1966)

and expresses notions of economy and efficiency. This engineering aesthetic fits with the popular image of engineers: practical, straight-talking, no-nonsense. Yet in recent years, cable-stayed bridges have had a liberating impact on the Functionalist engineering aesthetic. When engineers began exploiting the sculptural potential of cable-stayed bridges, a poetic genie was let out of the bottle.

Engineers quickly responded to the design possibilities offered by cable-stayed bridges. The first large-span cable-stayed bridge, the Strömsund Bridge in Sweden (designed by the German engineer Franz Dischinger), was opened in 1956 (63). It was an elegant, simple steel bridge that on first sight, looked a lot like a (then) more familiar suspension bridge, except that the cables supporting the deck were stretched straight rather than hung in a catenary curve between the pairs of top-braced towers. German designers soon established a look for cable-stayed bridges, based on their particular structural principles: that visually differentiated them from suspension bridges.

The Brücke Forsthausweg (64) was designed as a footbridge leading to the German Pavilion for the Brussels Expo of 1958 (and rebuilt to the original design in 1997 to span an autobahn in Germany). Expo 58 was the first major World's Fair after World War II and a proud celebration of European 'post-war' reconstruction. The Brücke Forsthausweg was a demonstration of German design and engineering ingenuity. The bridge consisted of a single mast-like steel pylon with cables stretching down on both sides to support an otherwise cantilevered steel beam. This use of a single pylon became one of the distinguishing structural features of many subsequent cable-stayed bridges.

In reducing the bridge to its elemental essentials, the designers (architects Egon Eiermann and Sep Ruf) visibly separated out the principal structural elements – pylon, beam and cables – painting them bright yellow to differentiate them from the footbridge deck, which was cantilevered off the beam and visually detached from it. Their design was also a display of statics (the balance of forces required to achieve equilibrium): the asymmetrical load of the cantilevered deck was counteracted by angling the foot of the pylon back under the deck; and the shorter end of the beam was tied down to counteract the greater load, at its longer end. As a rational and functional exposition of a cable-stayed bridge structure, the Brücke Forsthausweg soon became a model adopted by engineers all over the world.

When engineers began exploiting the sculptural potential of cable-stayed bridges, a poetic genie was let out of the bottle.

The Pont des îles, a cable-stayed bridge built 10 years later for the Montréal Expo 1967, might appear as heavy-handed (65). But it is a structure of its time, designed at the height of the Brutalist period of modern architecture. Its expressive muscularity points away from the accepted engineering canon of the time. Then, and for the previous 40 years, engineers had concentrated on achieving the lightest possible appearance for their bridges (even to the point of catastrophic collapse in the case of the Tacoma Narrows Bridge). They also desired a strictly rational and highly abstracted structural expressionism.

BRIDGE POETICS
Beaulieu, Trudeau et Associés had other expressive intentions in-mind in designing the Pont des îles. At each end and in mid-stream, there is a heavy concrete pier that

cradles the width of the bridge deck. The cradling arms of the central pier extend up beyond the level of the parapet to form a pair of freestanding pylons: the cable supports. On footpaths along the banks of the St Lawrence River, the bridge is viewed from below the level of the deck. The concrete deck, although visually massive, appears to float above the piers, restrained rather than supported by their cradling embrace. The only visible support seems to be the prestressed concrete beams under the mid-point of each span. These beams are unambiguously held up by the cables, a masterful and direct expression of how a cable-stayed structure works.

This inversion of the expected heuristic (that bridge structures should expressively be lightweight) is not the only canonical disruption. The two pylons are not rendered simply as structural elements. In ancient Egypt, to enter a pharaonic temple, one passed through a gateway formed by two pylons. This may be no more than a play on words, but engineers call the supporting towers of a cable-stayed bridge 'pylons'; and to enter either side of the Expo site, one must pass between the bridge's two central pylons: they are a gateway. To reinforce this poetic idea, the pylons are obelisk-shaped and rise, sculpted in concrete, out of the pier below. The designers of the Pont des îles disturbed the accepted premise 'that bridges should express no more that their functional attributes', and proposed 'instead that they might incorporate metaphor to convey poetic meaning'.

It is difficult to imagine concrete, which is so massive and monolithic, as a plastic material, but at the construction stage when it is a liquid, concrete is capable of taking the shape of any mould it is poured into. In the 1930s, Maillart exploited this plastic quality of concrete to achieve bridges of poetic structural clarity and great economy. Many engineers have used these same properties, first in the design of concrete bridges and then of cable-stayed bridge pylons. In the latter case, the concrete is contorted during construction to form rigid-framed pylons with complex structural geometries. Cable-stayed bridge designers have developed many variations on a limited number of geometric themes: pylons in the shapes of a capital A, H, I, a diamond-shaped double V and an inverted Y (66–70). The choice of one or another of these forms has depended on purely functional-structural considerations.

But it was in Montréal at Expo 67, and in front of fifty million visitors, that Beaulieu and Trudeau transcended purely functional-structural criteria, by using the plastic pre-nature of concrete, to sculpt the pylons into a metaphorical gateway. This was probably the moment when the engineer's poetic genie first escaped its bottle. Just when and who was next to subordinate functional-structural criteria to achieve sculptural and poetic effects in the design of bridges is hard to determine, though it was probably in Spain where, by 1978, the engineering firm of Carlos Fernández Casado had completed the beautiful Sancho el Mayor Bridge across the Ebro River (71).

It is a cable-stayed bridge with a single concrete pylon expressively raked backwards, like the anchorman at the end of a 'tug-of-war' rope resisting the countervailing forces of the team at the other end. The designers exploit the plastic nature of concrete with sculpted folds in the back-edge of the pylon, that split the anchoring backstays to form a pair of voluminous fan-shaped hyperbolic paraboloids. When discussing these backstays, the designers speak of their 'magical regard' for cables; and there is indeed something magical in the way the cables have turned a simple structural

66 A-type cable-stayed pylon: Severinsbrücke, Germany (1956–61)

67 H-type cable-stayed pylon: Bill Emerson Memorial Bridge, Mississippi River, Illinois, USA (2003)

68 I-type cable-stayed pylon: Rheinbrücke, Neuenkam, Germany (1971)

69 Double V-type cable-stayed pylon: Bhumibol Bridge, Bangkok, Thailand (2006)

70 Inverted Y-type cable-stayed pylon: Rama VIII Bridge, Bangkok, Thailand (2002)

71 Sancho el Mayor Bridge, Spain, designed by Carlos Fernández Casado (1978)

72 Sancho el Mayor Bridge, showing the split anchoring backstays that form a pair of voluminous fan-shaped hyperbolic paraboloids

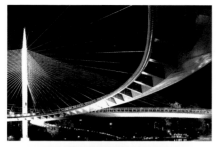

73 Manzanares River Footbridge, Madrid (2002), Carlos Fernández Casado Engineers

74 Quarto Ponte, Grand Canal, Venice, Italy (2008), designed by Santiago Calatrava

75 Quarto Ponte, Grand Canal, Venice

76 Footbridge Goathland Station, England

77 Typical railway footbridge

element into spatial experience: they form the open weave of an 'antechamber' one must pass through to reach the bridge and the country beyond (72).

FOOTBRIDGE RENAISSANCE

Bridge designers around the world now began to seriously explore the poetical and sculptural potential of bridges, and particularly footbridges. In Spain, the push was led by the Carlos Fernández Casado designers (73) and a few years later by the architect-engineer, Santiago Calatrava. Calatrava is significant for the way he uses metaphors from nature as catalysts for his structural designs: bird wings, animal skeletons, flowers and trees. He has also demonstrated that poetic expression is not limited to cable-stayed designs, but extends to other structural types. Calatrava's design for the Quarto Ponte across the Grand Canal in Venice (2008) is structurally a steel truss segmental arch, but poetically it suggests the skeletal ribbed forms of bird wings flying over the canal (74, 75).

Until the railways, most bridges were built with foot traffic in mind. Then from the early 19th-century, bridges were built primarily to carry trains and from the beginning of the 20th-century, motor vehicles. When bridges were built specifically for pedestrians – footbridges – their purpose was to remove people from traffic. The first of these were over railway lines, and initially they were little examples of engineering elegance (76), but later they became examples of utilitarian ugliness (77). For most of the 20th-century, footbridges (were built under the direction of traffic engineers) to prevent pedestrians from impeding the flow of traffic.

The renaissance of the footbridge can be traced back to the moment when urban traffic congestion threatened to strangle the life of cities, and when many city-dwellers put on their Nikes and took to the pavements and parks, on foot, to reclaim their cities from cars. Planners and politicians shifted focus from the efficient movement of traffic to thinking about the quality of life in cities. Design teams of urban planners, landscape architects, architects and civil engineers worked together. They recovered neglected industrial harbour, river and canal edges for public use with walkways and cycle paths; and on long narrow stretches of derelict and poorly-drained land – the sites of forgotten water courses – they laid out new linear parks, and the pleasure garden became a new design paradigm.

Water is a central feature of many new urban parks, and footbridges a necessary element. Footbridges are often the most visible piece of infrastructure in parks. Compared to bridges intended for heavy vehicle traffic, footbridges are by nature, lightweight structures with relatively undemanding spans, of a much smaller (and human) scale and relatively cheap to build: all factors that encouraged designers to experiment and to push poetic and structural boundaries.

Footbridge designs typically follow one of five structural typologies: arch, suspension, beam, truss and cable-stayed. To achieve an iconic status frequently expected of these bridges, designers creatively disturb structural conventions to produce large-scale sculptural effects or unexpected and novel interpretations of existing structural conventions. Many hundreds of these bridges have been built in the last 20 years. The handful of contemporary footbridges shown here are selected as examples:

Passerelle Simone de Beauvoir, Paris (2006), designed by architect Deitmar Feichtinger and the Eiffel company, is based on a steel lenticular truss (78). A historic version of this type of structure is Brunel's Royal Albert Bridge, Saltash (1853–59) (34).

Borneo-Sporenburg Bridge, Amsterdam (1998–2001), designed by landscape architects West 8, is a steel truss bridge based on a distorted segmental arch (79).

The tubular-steel truss railway footbridge at La Roche-sur-Yon, France (2010) is designed by architects Bernard Tschumi and Hugh Dutton (80, 81). The bridge relies on 'stressed skin' structural principles, in which the compression members (the regularly-spaced circular hoops) are localised and the tension members (the triangulated diagonals) are distributed across the surface of the tube.

Millennium Footbridge, London (1996–2000), designed by architects Foster Associates with Arup engineers and artist Anthony Caro, is a novel suspension-type bridge in which the suspension cables are, unusually, below the level of the deck (82).

Webb Bridge, Melbourne (2003), designed by architects Denton Corker Marshall with artist Robert Owen (83), is another tubular steel truss design based on a monocoque structure (similar to a 'stressed skin' structure, but with the compression and tension elements more equally spread across the surface of the structure).

. . . is a novel suspension-type bridge in which the suspension cables are, unusually, below the level of the deck

The Sundial Bridge, California (2004), designed by Santiago Calatrava, is a cable-stayed bridge (84) in which the single asymmetrical pylon is also the gnomon of a giant sundial (although the shadow cast by the bridge is exactly accurate on only one day a year, the summer solstice).

The circular footbridge across two canals in Aveiro, Portugal (2006), is a cable-stayed bridge with a geometrically sculpted, looped, inverted 'Y-shaped' pylon (85). The geometry of the circular bridge deck enables the three sides of the canals to be connected (86).

The BP Bridge, Chicago (2000–04), designed by architect Frank Gehry, is a welded steel box girder beam that forms a continuous ramp snaking its way from one side of a freeway to the other (87).

Langkawi Sky Bridge, Malaysia (2005), is yet another cable-stayed bridge with a single asymmetrical pylon from which the curving bridge deck is spectacularly suspended above the jungle (88).

78 Passerelle Simone de Beauvoir, Paris, France (2006), designed by architect Deitmar Feichtinger and the Eiffel company

79 Borneo-Sporenburg Bridge, Amsterdam, Holland (1998–2001), designed by landscape architects West 8

80 Railway footbridge, La Roche-sur-Yon, France (2010), designed by architects Bernard Tschumi and Hugh Dutton

81 Railway footbridge, La Roche-sur-Yon, France

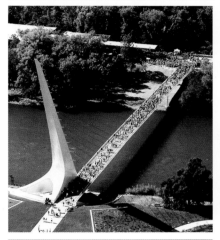

At normal traffic speed, crossing a bridge in a car is no more than a fleeting experience (if experienced at all) mediated through the enclosed and controlled environment of a car, in which even the view, screened by security rails, is largely withheld. For a pedestrian crossing a bridge at a walking pace, there is time to take in the experience of the views and the weather. There is even time to feel (however subliminally) the pleasure of being on a journey and momentarily suspended (literally and metaphysically) between two worlds.

The poetics of the journey are evident in several of these footbridge examples, and together they indicate the extent to which the contemporary footbridge has become the locus of the most poetical design experiments. And it is along this particular trajectory of contemporary bridge design, that we locate the Kurilpa Bridge in Brisbane.

For a pedestrian crossing a bridge at a walking pace, there is time to take in the experience of the views and the weather.

82 Millennium Footbridge, London, England (1996–2000), designed by architects Foster Associates with Arup engineers and artist Anthony Caro

83 Webb Bridge, Melbourne, Australia (2003) designed by architects Denton Corker Marshall with artist Robert Owen

84 Sundial Bridge, California, USA (2004), designed by Santiago Calatrava

85 Circular footbridge, Aveiro, Portugal (2006)

86 Circular footbridge, Aveiro, Portugal (2006)

87 BP Bridge, Chicago, USA (2000–04), designed by architect Frank Gehry

88 Langkawi Sky Bridge, Malaysia (2005)

THE ARCHITECT

Needless to say, Kurilpa Bridge was a dream commission, one that presented unprecedented design challenges, but also the potential to dramatically enhance the experience of Brisbane by foot and cycle: as it should be for a subtropical city.

The idea of a link in its location was conceptualised nearly a decade earlier when we were competing for the Brisbane Magistrates Court on what was then called Queensland Place (See page 40). At that time, we envisaged how this link could connect South Bank and the Cultural Precinct across the river and up into the newly formed Roma Street Parklands. However, this would not be the bridge we would design next – it was the Goodwill Bridge, further downstream.

The Goodwill Bridge was the result of an architectural competition. Its location was vehemently opposed by apartment residents on the South Bank side who believed that the bridge would affect their privacy, among other concerns. Some people argued that it would blight the serenity of the river by its visual impact. These concerns caused a repositioning of the bridge into the Maritime Museum precinct, and a development of the design to minimise its visual presence.

The ability to create, some 10 years later, a more dynamic and evocative bridge at the Kurilpa end of the same river reach, is testimony to changing Brisbane perceptions. The Kurilpa Bridge is, in our view, a potent statement of our city's growing self-confidence. It is not that its design doesn't have detractors, but as Haig Beck and Jackie Cooper point out in their text, unfamiliar forms generate metaphors and analogies to things which are familiar. So far, we have heard of the bridge being likened to a bunch of old 'Hills Hoists', and to a game of 'Pick-up-sticks'. To us, as designers, it offers deeper meanings and an experience of the river that is much enhanced by its particular design.

We had no metaphors in mind during conceptualisation. It is also important to recognise that the 'tensegrity' structure originated in the mind of Arup's Tristram Carfrae due to the fact that all conventional typologies we considered – arches, tubes, box trusses and suspension structures – could not be easily resolved in this location. We needed a thin deck, for example, so that the length of the ramp down on the south side would not 'consume' Kurilpa Park. We needed a structure that would integrally support a continuous canopy, and would effortlessly span across the motorway into Tank Street on the city side. And we wanted a structure that did not over-scale the Gallery of Modern Art.

It was, however, not only for these reasons that we embraced Carfrae's idea. When we discovered that a major exponent of tensegrity structures was an artist – the American sculptor Kenneth Snelson – we saw synergies with the neighbouring Gallery of Modern Art, and a larger vision that the bridge could symbolise the fusion of art, science and technology, this fusion we believe as being seminal to Queensland's future economy and cultural vitality.

Even more inspiring, however, was the opportunity that the tensegrity structure offered, unlike any other bridge typology, to change formations along the journey – as if the bridge itself actually suggested movement. If we had evoked a metaphor perhaps it would have been that of a dance momentarily frozen in time. That aside, we were excited that a bridge of this type could generate a dynamic experience for pedestrian and cyclist, its projecting decks affording spectacular views along the river, and creating intriguing urban spaces in the city.

... we saw synergies with the Gallery, and a larger vision that the bridge could symbolise the fusion of art, science and technology

If we had evoked a metaphor perhaps it would have been that of a dance momentarily frozen in time.

Kurilpa Bridge was procured in a different way to the Goodwill Bridge. Instead of a pure architectural competition, the Queensland Government decided to require a consortium of builders, architects and engineers where the contractor would commit to a predetermined construction value. This process avoided the type of contest where tenderers bid on the cheapest solution, rather than on design and creativity.

It was a process that allowed the team to demonstrate Queensland's progressiveness not only in design and engineering, but in construction. Once commissioned, this team also included the Department of Public Works as an integral member, especially in navigating the design through a myriad of agencies and authorities. The process placed enormous responsibility upon Baulderstone, who not only embraced our unconventional vision from the beginning, but who became integral to the design process.

Teams comprise of individuals and it is their continuous collaboration throughout that defines the success of Kurilpa Bridge – Paul Stathis and Phil Reed in particular from Baulderstone, Project Director Jeff Griffin from the Department of Public Works and Project Manager Glenn Bourner from RCP, Ian Ainsworth from Arup, and Antony Scott-Pegum and Casey Vallance from Cox Rayner. These people and others worked virtually hand-in-hand for the 36 months that the bridge took from conception to opening, from agonising over computer impact tests received from London to standing at 2am on the motorway to test the lighting systems. Can we also acknowledge the concreters and steel workers who epitomise the pursuit of quality in the many tradespeople who saw the bridge as a mission.

Kurilpa Bridge is sited at the main crossing point where Aboriginal people waded across the river along sand bars formed at the bend. These were the Jagera and Turrbal people, whose journeys extended to the Bunya Mountains and the Conondale Ranges. Their stories are told in texts inscribed along the bridge through to Kurilpa Park, that was a significant meeting place and a neutral ground for the tribes. The enthusiastic embrace of Kurilpa Bridge by the Jagera and Turrbal people is the final rewarding piece in the story of Kurilpa Bridge's evolution.

Michael Rayner, Cox Rayner Architects

Kurilpa Bridge is sited at the main crossing point where Aboriginal people waded across the river

THE ENGINEER

Bridges are very special to engineers. Their structure is visible for all to see rather than being hidden behind walls and ceilings, as is the case for most buildings. Bridges offer engineers the opportunity to display their craft and creativity. In the past, it was common for engineers to be solely responsible for both the structural design and the aesthetics of bridges. Even today there are some in the engineering fraternity who believe that structural efficiency and classic structural forms are the only valid considerations when designing bridges. Arup, with its philosophy of holistic design and sustainability, takes the view that there are many more factors in the design of important parts of the urban fabric than structural efficiency, and that the best results come from combining the talents of a range of collaborators, including architects and constructors.

The Kurilpa Bridge provides a wonderful example of how a truly collaborative approach from a team with diverse and complementary skills can produce a result which is much richer, than could be produced by structural engineers working in isolation. This is not to diminish the structural engineering accomplishment: the use of tensegrity in a major structure has been a holy grail for architects and engineers around the world for a century, and the successful completion of the Kurilpa Bridge represents a genuine world first. To overcome the technical challenges posed by the difficult site and the innovative form and to do so on time and budget is a remarkable achievement and one of which, all involved in the project can be proud.

At the outset of the Kurilpa Bridge journey, Arup realised that the nature of the site demanded a structure that would sit comfortably beside the Gallery of Modern Art building, whose appearance and amenity would draw pedestrians and cyclists across the river, and that would build on the development of Brisbane as a contemporary river city. Arup teamed up with Cox Rayner and Baulderstone intent on developing a design that would ensure that the team would win the design competition and the right to build the bridge, and also deliver a design that could be safely and efficiently constructed.

With an unprecedented structural form and the innumerable challenges posed by building over the river and the busy roads on the north bank: every aspect of the design had to be developed from first principles, then comprehensively analysed and tested. In addition, to conventional structural engineering: the structural design process included wind tunnel testing and computer simulation, design and testing of bespoke deck dampers and mast dampers to ensure comfort and safety under dynamic loading from crowds and wind, and sophisticated computer modelling of each and every step of the erection process. This construction 'dress rehearsal' ensured that the carefully designed set of thousands of prefabricated precast concrete, steel and cable components would fit together, with every part of the completed structure in the correct theoretical position, and every cable correctly pretensioned by the weight of the structure.

Ian Ainsworth, Arup

. . . the use of tensegrity in a major structure has been a holy grail for architects and engineers around the world for a century

THE CONTRACTOR

The creative partnership of Cox Rayner, Arup and Baulderstone produced the world's first tensegrity pedestrian and cycle bridge, a bold fusion of art and science that features a geometric array of cables and flying steel spars. Building Kurilpa Bridge was a construction marvel and it came with its own set of challenges. The bridge had to be constructed in a tightly controlled environment in the central CBD; over a thriving commercial and recreational river; and across the busiest road corridor in Queensland – with little disruption and zero obstruction. The erection of the superstructure needed to be planned with the utmost precision to ensure that the bridge would end up in the correct position when the thousands of prefabricated pieces (cables, masts, spars and deck beams) were bolted together.

When constructing large complex structures, there are two basic approaches that can be taken to ensure that the completed project has the correct geometry. The first: is to constantly monitor the position of the structure during construction, making adjustments along the way. The second: is to accurately prefabricate all the components, and to confirm before building commences (called 'scenario planning') that connecting all of the components together without adjustment, will produce the final geometry. For Kurilpa Bridge, the complexity of the structure and the time available for erection meant that the second option had to be taken, with the bridge builders forced to rely on the accuracy of the designers' predictions.

There were no opportunities for taking up any slack in the cables or lengthening or shortening the masts after the components were erected. The hollow steel masts were prefabricated to exact lengths, and when erecting them, the builders had to locate the top end of each at a specific point in space. The many steel cables fixed to the tops of the masts were manufactured in the UK to specified individual lengths, and checked just prior to erection, with the knowledge that they couldn't be adjusted after erection.

As the bridge was built, it progressively cantilevered out over the river. The bridge deck was prefabricated in 12.8 metre segments craned into place from a barge moored in the river. Baulderstone's project manager, Paul Stathis, remembers, 'We were building the bridge piece by piece, and at times, night by night. With the exception of the bridge deck and the crossbeams (the horizontal tensegrity masts), every element of the structure was different, in a sense, random. However, the building process was definitely not speculative or random: each step was planned'.

Stephen Green, Baulderstone

Building Kurilpa Bridge was a construction marvel and it came with its own set of challenges.

THE NEIGHBOUR

It is a pleasurable fact that part of my working day is spent in the airy interiors of the Gallery of Modern Art on Brisbane's South Bank. From large, glass-enclosed 'verandah' spaces at the front of the building, clear views of the Brisbane River and the north bank of the CBD are revealed. Prominent in this cityscape is the sinuous line of the Kurilpa Bridge, via which many of our visitors approach the Gallery and surrounding cultural precinct. By both day and night, the bridge creates an impression of constant movement and animation, with its vertical elements seemingly cart-wheeling between the Gallery and the western edge of the CBD. It is energetic and kinetic, and complements the spirit of the modern and contemporary art that the Gallery exhibits.

Prior to the redevelopment of the northern end of South Bank and the construction of the bridge, Kurilpa Point was a rather neglected area, although one with important cultural significance for this area's traditional owners, the Jagera and Turrbal people. Originally a social gathering place, Kurilpa Point's latent potential as an area of significant public presence and thoroughfare has been realised anew with the Kurilpa Bridge.

Once the bridge was opened, the re-energising of the western end of the CBD has begun to take place, with new connections forged between the transit hub and parkland of Roma Street and the South Bank and Brisbane's West End. Kurilpa Point is a thriving node of social activity, which the Gallery and cultural precinct both serve and benefit from.

The Kurilpa Bridge is a contemporary landmark appropriate for an evolving and relatively young city. Its design language is bold, forthright and playful. The governing structural principle of tensegrity allows a lightness of form expressive of a subtropical, youthful city, yet also provides robustness of structure to ensure a lasting landmark as the city develops into the future. It is through the contribution of such infrastructure as the Kurilpa Bridge that cities can be reborn and reshaped, and new channels of thoroughfare, communication and energy activated.

Tony Ellwood, Director, Queensland Art Gallery

By both day and night, the bridge creates an impression of constant movement and animation, with its vertical elements seemingly cart-wheeling between the Gallery and the western edge of the CBD.

THE
PROCESS

The Kurilpa Bridge was originally entitled the Tank Street Bridge because of its chosen alignment which enabled the bridge to connect into and through the new justice precinct to the city's Roma Street Parklands, connecting them across the river to the South Bank Parkland.

The Queensland Government's intention to construct the bridge dates back to December 2004. Its announcement was made by the then Premier Peter Beattie with a budget of $63.3 million approved in the 2005/6 Capital Works State Budget to be delivered by the Department of Public Works.

The aim of the bridge was principally to link the Brisbane CBD to the new Gallery of Modern Art and State Library in the cultural precinct. However, it was also recognised as forming a critical part of the city centre's pedestrian and cycle network, that also includes the Goodwill Bridge to the south.

It was felt that its location adjoining the State's major cultural facilities demanded a dramatic design that could become synonymous with a subtropical city prioritising walking and cycling.

To create the best opportunity for such a design, the Government staged a competition requiring consortia of contractor, architect and engineer to submit designs capable of being built for the budget. This process differed from the conventional 'design' and 'construct' tender, in that the budget was set, and consortia were requested to create the best design they could to that budget.

Following the initial call for submissions in October 2006, three consortia were shortlisted. The submissions were evaluated by a panel comprising of representatives of the Department of Public Works, the Government Architects Office, South Bank Corporation and Brisbane City Council. The successful team of Baulderstone Hornibrook Queensland Pty Ltd, Cox Rayner Architects and Arup was announced by the Premier on 5 March 2007 as the preferred tenderer.

Using a Managing Contractor framework, the Department of Public Works and its advisors then worked with Baulderstone and its design team to develop the design to meet the technical and cost parameters. This process enabled what was an unprecedented bridge design to be accepted by the Government. Based upon it, the Department and the Contractor entered a standard Lump Sum Design and Construct Contract.

On 1 October 2007, the Premier announced Baulderstone as the successful contractor with its design team of Cox Rayner Architects and Arup. It opened almost exactly two years later, on 4 October 2009, justifying the process of design and procurement in its adherence to the original concept.

Max Smith
Deputy Director-General, Works
Department of Public Works

THE PROJECT TEAM AND LEADERS

THE PROJECT SUPPLIERS AND SUBCONTRACTORS

CLIENT
Queensland Government, Department of Public Works
Max Smith
Jeff Griffin
John Bellas

DESIGN AND CONSTRUCT MANAGER
Baulderstone
Stephen Green
Paul Stathis
Phil Reed
Nick Ayres

ARCHITECT
Cox Rayner Architects
Michael Rayner
Philip Cox
Antony Scott-Pegum
Casey Vallance

STRUCTURAL, CIVIL AND GEOTECHNICAL CONSULTANT
ELECTRICAL AND LIGHTING CONSULTANT
MECHANICAL AND HYDRAULIC CONSULTANT
Arup
Ian Ainsworth
Tristram Carfrae
Peter Burnton

LANDSCAPE CONSULTANT
Gamble McKinnon Green
Andrew Green

SIGNAGE
Dot Dash
Mark Ross

ARTWORK INSTALLATION
Urban Art Projects
Matthew Tobin
Daniel Tobin

DISABILITY CONSULTANT
Eric Martin + Associates
Eric Martin

PROJECT MANAGER
RCP
Russell Martoo
Glenn Bourner

COXRAYNER

ARUP

Access
Waco Kwikform

Anti Graffiti Application
Graffiti Gone

Bearings
Ludowici Aust Pty Ltd
Trelleborg

Building Products
Ancon Building Products

Chemical Products
BASF

Concrete
Boral Concrete

Drilling of Boreholes
Austress Mernard

Electrical
Stowe Australia

General Tools
South East Fasteners

Grouting
Building Solutions

Labour
ART Constructions
Leckton Pty
Paul Rizzo Concreting
Starlight Engineering

Land Piling
AFS Solutions

Lighting
ECC Lighting

Marine Piling Wide Form Formwork
Waterways

Metalwork
Stoddart

Plant
BRS Civil
Carsburg Earthmoving
Hanchard Crane Hire
Hydrovac
Specialised Concrete Pumping
Universal Cranes

Plumbing
Alston Plumbing

Post-Tensioning
Austress Freyssinet

Precast Concrete
Precast Concrete Products

Regrading
Brisbane City Works

Reinforcement
Smorgan

Safety Equipment
Australian Health & Safety Supplies

Signage
Artcraft Pty Ltd
Insigniature Signs

Stability Assessor
Sealife Designs

Stainless Steel Cabling
Bridon

Structural Steelworks
Beenleigh Steel

Surveillance
Barry Bros Specialised Services

Surveyor
Lyntons Surveyors
Soil Surveys

Trafffic Control
Traffic Management Services

Traffic Engineering
McCormick Rankin Cagney

Tree Maintenance
Arbor Australis

Vacuum Excavation
Vac-u-digga

Verification
Cardno

Vibration Monitoring
Heilig and Partners

Waterproofing
Danlaid

Wind Tunnel Testing
BMT Fluid Mechanics
Mel Consultants Pty Ltd

Length of main span
128 metres

Overall length of footway (including ramps)
425 metres

Height of underside of deck above high water
11.4 metres

Tons of steel
560 tonnes

Kilometres of steel tensegrity cable
6.8 kilometres

Cubic metres of concrete
500m³

Range of lengths of steel compression members
(the tensegrity 'masts')
14 to 17m and 18m to 33m

Number of solar panels
**84 providing approximately 75% per cent
of all power and lighting requirements
for the bridge**

Number of LED lights
144

Number of days on site to build
431

Average number of users per week in 2011
30,000

Project value
$63,300,000

Number of names suggested for the naming of the
bridge
1,130

Concrete piers and abutments
Off-form coloured concrete

Bridge deck
Coloured concrete

Main canopy
**Paint-finished compressed fibre cement
and powdercoated aluminium**

Secondary canopies
Powdercoated aluminium

Masts, spars, canopy beams,
deck support framing and edge beams
Steel with acrylic polysiloxane paint

Cables
Galvanised and stainless steel cables

Balustrade infill panels
Hot-dipped galvanised steel

Balustrade stanchions
**Hot-dipped galvanised steel
with thermoplastic paint**

Anti-throw screens
**Woven stainless steel mesh in
galvanised steel angle frame**

Glazing to canopy and privacy screens
Low iron toughened laminated glass

PHOTOGRAPHERS

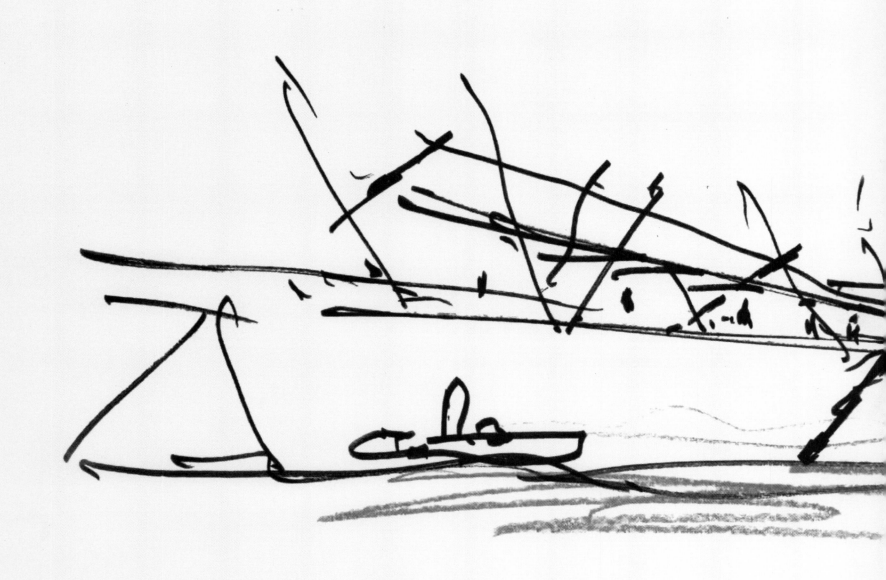